It is

"the worst time

to be famous"

John Travolta, 2013

Only

"if you're

living a lie!"

Robert Randolph, 2013

Travoltanized

(coined by Robert Randolph 2010)

Adj 1. Travoltanized---to become invisible.
"After turning Travolta down for sex one may find themselves 'Travoltanized'
2. To punish or destroy on a whim.
3. To make a victim for no good reason.
4. Sexualized exploitation of the working class, mainly masseurs and helpless male workers of all ages.

Tracking Travolta

Through the

"Massage Scandal"

and more

Robert Randolph

The proceeds

from

Tracking Travolta

and

You'll Never Spa In This Town Again

are being

DONATED

to the

LGBT

Community!

Copyright © 2014 Robert Randolph All rights reserved.

ISBN-13:978-0692254745

ISBN-10:0692254749

CONTENTS

Pg-1	John Travolta/Robert Randolph Quote
Pg-2	"Travoltanized" Definition
Pg-3	Tracking Travolta Through the "Massage Scandal" & more
Pg-4	Proceeds from books
Pg-5	Polygraph Tested Reading material "CERTIFIED"
Pg-6	Contents
Pg-7	Contents
Pg-8	Contents
Pg-9	Contents
Pg-10	Opening Statement
Pg-11	Dedication
Pg-12	Polygraph Examination
Pg-13	The Examiner
Pg-14	Lie Detector Test
Pg-15	Lie Detector Test
Pg-16	Lie Detector Test
Pg-17	Lie Detector Test
Pg-18	Lie Detector Results
Pg-19-25	Author's Notes
Pg-26-29	Introduction
Pg-30-37	Travolta Encounter Witnessed Sexual Hookup. ---March 29, 2013, 5:45 Pictures Taken
Pg-38	Email Definition
Pg-39-43	Travolta Sex Encounter Email. ---March 28, 2013, 6:30 PM. Pictures Taken
Pg-44	Section 2010 Mini Update
Pg-45	Carrie Fisher Quote Regarding Travolta's sexuality and My Book "You'll Never Spa In This Town Again"
Pg-46	Travolta Sex Encounter Email
Pg-47	My Email Response Back
Pg-48-52	Travolta Sex Encounter Email: "John's Secret North Of The Border Lover"
Pg-53-55	The Very First Email I Received
Pg-56-58	Travolta Sex Encounter Email: "From The Wife Of One Of Travolta's Lovers"
Pg-59-60	Email From Employee At Summit Hotel: "Travolta's Running All Over Vancouver Looking For Dick"
Pg-60-61	Travolta Encounter Email From Vancouver Canada
Pg-61-62	Travolta Sex Encounter Email
Pg-63	Travolta Sex Encounter Email: "Travolta's Masturbating In His Car"
Pg-64	Email From City Spa Employee
Pg-65	Travolta Sex Encounter Email: "Travolta's Getting It On In The Russian Room"
Pg-66	Travolta Encounter Email: "Travolta's Banned From Brooks Spa"
Pg-67	Travolta Encounter Email From Employee At Hotel Sofitel: "Travolta's Getting Naked For Room Service"
Pg-68	Email From Bruce Headrick: "Best Friends Back In The Day With Paul Barresi, J.T.'s Boyfriend"
Pg-69-71	Tell Secrets, Tell no Lies

Pg-71	Travolta Encounter Email: Chris Williams "Massaged Travolta For Over A Decade Before He Was Thrown Out Like The Trash"
Pg-72-79	Chris Williams
Pg-80-81	Chris Williams/Robert Randolph Facebook Correspondence
Pg-82	Email Regarding The Murder Of Ronnie Chasen --- "Travolta's Old PR Gal"
Pg-82-84	The Murder Of Ronnie Chasen
Pg-85	Email From Mark Riccardi "Travolta's EXCLUSIVE STUNT DOUBLE" In Thirteen Films
Pg-86	My Email Response back To Mark Riccardi
Pg-87-95	Mark Riccardi
Pg-96	Email Regarding Travolta's Five Pages Of Lies About Me To Gawker.com
Pg-97-101	The "ACTUAL" Letter To Gawker... Sorry It Is Not That Clear... If You Zoom In, You Can Read It.
Pg-102	My Attorney's Response Letter
Pg-103-104	The "ACTUAL" Letter From My Attorney To Travolta's
Pg-105-107	Emails From Gawker.com and Myself, Setting Up The Interview: "The Secret Sex Life Of John Travolta"
Pg-108- 109	The Secret Sex Life Of John Travolta
Pg-110	Email Of Support
Pg-111	Email Of Support
Pg-112	Email Of Support
Pg-113	Two Emails Of Support
Pg-114-116	My Email To Gloria Allred
Pg-117-118	Email Reply From Gloria Allred
Pg-118-121	Gloria Allred
Pg-123-124	Section 2011 Mini Update
Pg-125	Joan Edwards Quote: "Travolta's Personal Secretary For Sixteen Years Referring To His Sexuality"
Pg-126	Travolta Sexual Assault Encounter Against Room Service Employee Fabian Zanzi On Royal Carribbean Cruise Line, June 7, 2009
Pg-127	Email From Fabian Asking Me For Help
Pg-128	My Email Response To Fabian
Pg-129-136	Fabian Zanzi "The Cruise Ship Worker" Who Lost Everything Because Of Travolta
Pg-137	Travolta Sex Encounter Email: "Women Kills Herself Over Her Husband's Affair With Travolta"
Pg-138	Travolta Sex Encounter Email: "Travolta's Having Sex At Wilshire Spa"
Pg-139-141	Travolta Sex Encounter Email: "Man Witnesses Travolta Getting Oral Sex At Studio 54"
Pg-141-143	Travolta Sex Encounter Email: July 15, 2006, "Man Gets STD From Travolta"
Pg-144	Email of Support
Pg-145	Travolta Sex Encounter Email: "Travolta Observed Having Sex At Century Spa By A Member"
Pg-146	Travolta Sex Encounter Email: "Travolta Is Witnessed Having Sex With Mario"

Pg-147	Email Of Support
Pg-148	Email Of Support
Pg-149	Email Of Support
Pg-150	Travolta Sex Encounter Email: "Ritz Carlton Dana Point"
Pg-151	Email of Support
Pg-152	My Response Back
Pg-153	Response from Previous Email of Support
Pg-154	Warning Email From Scientologist
Pg-155	Warning Email From Scientologist
Pg-156-159	Scientology
Pg-160	Section 2012 Mini Update
Pg-161	Actress Rashida Jones Quote: "Urging Travolta To Come "Out" Already!
Pg-162	Email From Attorney Michael Bressler
Pg-163-164	The Attorney From Chicago
Pg-165	Email From Attorney Okorie Okorocha
Pg-166	My Email Reply To Okorie
Pg-167-169	Okorie Okorocha
Pg-170-184	Travolta Sexual Assault Encounter Email From Victim "John Doe 1", His Emails To Me And My Responses Back To Him
Pg-185-190	John Doe # 1
Pg-191-194	My Book "You'll Never Spa In This Town Again" Release " February 18, 2012, Travolta's Birthday"
Pg-195-197	Carrie Fisher
Pg-198-208	My Email To My Attorney Sarah Golden regarding My Witness List For Trial And Her Replies
Pg-209-212	Suing John Travolta And Marty Singer
Pg-213-217	Emails From TMZ And My Replies Back To Them
Pg-218-220	TMZ
Pg-221	Travolta Sex Encounter Email From Man Claiming To Be Doug Gotterba's EX Boyfriend
Pg-222-227	Doug Gotterba
Pg-228-230	Email From My Attorney Sarah Golden Regarding "Filing My And Fabian's Law Suit Against Travolta"
Pg-231-238	"Tracking Travolta 3" Vince And Ryan's Story… S & M Kinky!!
Pg-239	Travolta Sex Encounter Email: "Man Has Sex Three Times With Travolta"
Pg-240	Travolta Sex Encounter Email: "Travolta Is Witnessed Over A Ten Year Period Having Sex at City Spa"
Pg-241	Email Regarding Travolta's Old Manager Bob LeMond: "Travolta's Reps Blame The Gay Rumors Because His Agent Bob Was Gay"
Pg-242	Travolta Sex Encounter Email In Toronto: "While Filming Hairspray, Travolta Falls In Love With A Man On Set"
Pg-243	Email regarding Allan Carr, The Man Responsible For Putting Travolta In Grease
Pg-244	Email From John Doe #1
Pg-245-246	Emails Of Support

Pg-247	My Email Response Back
Pg-248-249	Amazing Email Of Support
Pg-250	Email From Man In Rio De Janero
Pg-251	Email Regarding "John REVOLTA"
Pg-252	Email From My Attorney Sarah
Pg-253	Email From My Attorney Sarah Regarding A Letter She Received From Travolta's Attorneys
Pg-254	My Email Response Back To Her
Pg-255-256	Email Letter From Travolta's Attorney To My Attorney Sarah:"It's Funny"
Pg-257-259	My Attorney's Response Letter Back To Opposing Counsel: "It's Funny, Too!"
Pg-260	Section 2013 Mini Update
Pg-261	Actress/Comedian Margret Cho's Quote Regarding Travolta's Sexuality
Pg-262-266	Joey Travolta "The True Star Of The Family!"
Pg-267-270	Jett Travolta
Pg-271-274	James Gandolfini
Pg-275-277	Queen Latifah TV Show Debut... First Guest Travolta
Pg-278	L. Ron Quote
Pg-279	John Travolta Quote
Pg-280	Coming Soon: Hitler's secret LGBT Holocaust
Pg-281-286	Travolta Encounter: "Flash Back To 2001, The Number One Reason I Never Had Sex With Travolta"
Pg-287-288	Travolta Sex Encounter: "He Has The Dirt On Travolta's Latest Boyfriend"
Pg-289-290	Travolta Sex Encounter: "Man From Santa Monica Had Sex Twice With Travolta"
Pg-291-292	Email Regarding A "Blind Gossip" Item... Travolta? Of Course!
Pg-293	My Email Response Back
Pg-294	Marty Singer's Quote About His Client Travolta: "Not Even Once Would John Do Such A Thing In A Spa"
Pg-295	The End For Now!
Pg-296-299	Acknowledgements

OPENING STATEMENT

To be a victim of a sexual assault is bad enough... But to have nowhere to turn because the assaulter is a movie star... With ties to a scary religion .... Is even worse... I was a victim of sexual assault too, many years ago..

I was no longer a victim when I kicked my assaulter's ass!!

John Travolta and his crazy attorneys have no power over me.

And they have no power over you...

If you have the truth on your side...

Author Robert Randolph

DEDICATION…

This book is dedicated to all the men that turned to me for help regarding their sexual situations with the actor John Travolta. Many of these victims had read about my upcoming book "You'll Never Spa In This Town Again" and sought me out for advice.

Some were going through current, sexual assault problems with Travolta, and others were asking me for help on longstanding sexual issues with the actor.

I was beyond shocked, to hear from so many men, that had been through such horrible sexual situations with the movie star.

I am proud that I am the man who has lifted the veil/towel on John Travolta and his predator ways of seeking out sex in public spas and now, the world knows, too.

To all of Travolta's victims of sexual assault or unwanted sexual advances, "I say go straight to your local police department if you find yourself at the end of one of his assaults, and report it."

To all the victims, this book is dedicated to you!

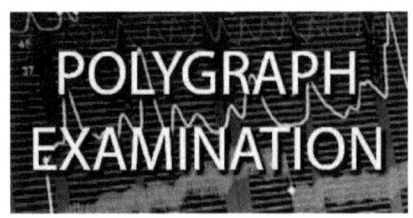

I think of myself as a new breed of writer, where my books are completely based on the truth, and I back that truth up with a polygraph examination in the beginning of all my books.

I feel the truth is much more important than perfect grammar or experience with writing books. I have found that most people, if given the chance, can handle the truth, and if given a choice, they would prefer it. For many years now, we have all been reading the edited, cut down, celebrity-approved version of the truth when it comes to their lives.

I am proud to be a new breed of truth tellers that will bring you the truth at all costs. Or at least, I can start my book with a lie detector test to try and show you this is a place where you are going to be reading the truth, not fiction. I challenged anyone to prove me to be a liar with my first book *"You'll Never Spa In This Town Again"*, in particular, John Travolta, he never took me up on that challenge and he never sued me for defamation of character or anything else.

I make the same challenge to Travolta or anyone else who may want to question whether this book is fact or fiction.

Sincerely,

Robert Randolph

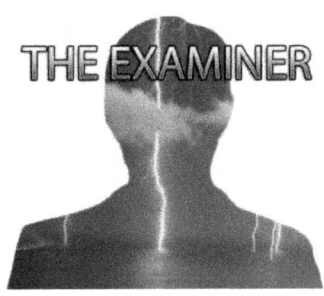

When the time came to do the polygraph test or "Lie Detector Test", if you prefer, I decided to go with a completely new examiner, I did not want to go back to the same one, for the sole reason that I did not want it to look like I was trying to make it easier on me. Here in Los Angeles where I live, I am lucky to have many of the world's top examiners practicing right here locally, so choosing a new examiner was not hard at all to do.

This polygraph examiner is a top expert in his field, and is well respected around the globe. He has administered over ten thousand examinations in his lengthy career, spanning four decades.

After spending twenty years in New York as a top consultant and examiner for many of the Fortune 500 companies, he was persuaded to move to California to pursue his profession of polygraph examinations. Shortly after arriving in Beverly Hills, he found himself sought out by the stars, attorneys, cheating husbands, and wives, and was a regular fixture on the daytime TV circuit for many years, performing his Polygraph exams on television.

He had just the background I was looking to find, after all, the first examiner for my book YNSITTA was really qualified, and I would accept no less from the new guy.

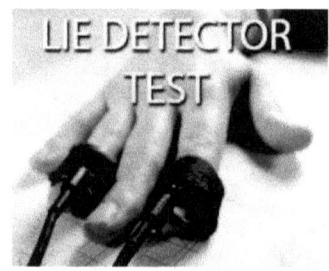

1. On March 29, 2013 did you witness John Travolta at Lyons spa in LA receiving a blow job? **Yes**

2. Is Travolta still frequenting the spas you wrote about in your first book YNSITTA? **Yes**

3. Do you have documented proof Mr. Travolta is still having sex in spas? **Yes**

4. Did Travolta threaten you when you ran into him at Lyons Spa? **Yes**

5. Did Mark Riccardi, Travolta's Exclusive stunt double in thirteen films with the star, reveal shocking secrets and XXX sex stories with you? **Yes**

6. Did Travolta payout to Fabian Zanzi a settlement due to his sexual assault on the cruise ship? **Yes**

7. Did you Robert Randolph help facilitate this settlement for Fabian Zanzi ? **Yes**

8. Are you aware of other men that are considering filing law suits against the actor? **Yes**

9. Did the men that are thinking about suing Travolta give you the details of the assaults? **Yes**

10. Did you take pictures of Travolta on your March 29, 2013 encounter that you reported to the police? **Yes**

11. Have you been contacted by past and present employees of the Travoltas? **Yes**

12. Did these employees share shocking stories with you? **Yes**

13. Do you plan on writing a book based on what the employees told you? **Yes**

14. Have you been contacted by many of Travolta's fellow actors? **Yes**

15. Were these celebrities supportive of you? **Yes**

16. Have any of these celebrities made their own public statement about Travolta's sexuality? **Yes**

17. Have any of the celebrities that contacted you told you they would come forward as a witness for you regarding Travolta's lies about his sexuality? **Yes**

18. Did you do anything to alter the original emails that were sent to you other than concealing most of the sender's information for privacy reasons? **No**

19. In your opinion is Travolta a sex addict? **Yes**

20. Do you hope he gets the medical attention he needs for his sex addiction? **Yes**

21. Are you still being bullied and receiving death threats regarding Travolta? **Yes**

22. Is John Travolta a homosexual? **Yes**

23. Is Travolta lying to the world and all his fans about who he really is? **Yes**

24. Is everything in your book true? **Yes**

25. Do you hope in some way by spreading this truth about Travolta's sexuality that you can help young LGBTs **Yes.**

26. Did you take a meeting with Sarah Golden, Esq and Servando Timbol, Esq Fabian Zanzi's attorney's, where they gave you the exact settlement amount Travolta paid out? **Yes.**

27. Did you record the settlement meeting to prove you are telling the truth and as proof, Sarah divulged all the details to you? **Yes.**

28. Did Sarah Golden share with you an extremely disturbing conversation she had with Linda Goldman, John Travolta's attorney? **Yes. (more later)**

29. If Travolta had done the right thing and paid Fabian a proper settlement so he could rebuild his life, would you have written further about Fabian? **No.**

30. Did Sarah tell you all the details of the settlement from Travolta and give you the settlement package? **Yes.**

31. Is your intention with this book to help spread awareness of the hypocrisy in Hollywood and its leading homosexual stars? **Yes.**

32. Are you hoping Travolta will look at his actions and change his behavior? **Yes.**

33. Did Travolta pay a settlement of $20,000 to Fabian Zanzi, due to his actions on the Royal Caribbean cruise ship? **Yes.**

34. Do you have ALL the documents to prove this? **Yes.**

35. Will you be releasing these documents? Yes.

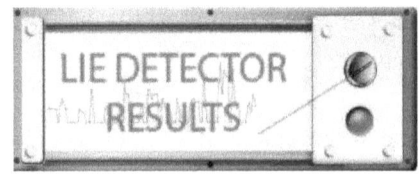

Conclusion:

It is the opinion of this examiner after carefully reviewing the polygraph charts of the subject (Robert Randolph) that there was absolutely no indication of deception during the polygraph examination that was conducted at my office in August 2014. This was taken from the report of the polygraph examiner I met with in 2014.

Now of course, I could write anything here I wanted to, but I didn't. The polygraph examinations that I provide at the beginning of my books are there so my readers can have a sense that I am telling the truth to them, and that I am willing to take a lie detector test to prove it. The results are on file with the office of the examiner. Of course, I have these reports in my possession as well, and will produce them if needed.

This is my way of showing I am telling the truth!

"I challenge John Travolta to sit down side by side with me and get a polygraph together and see who is telling the truth!"

AUTHOR'S NOTES

Don't you just hate it, when you're reading a Hollywood biography about one of your favorite stars and they're not alive to defend themselves? Me, too!

Especially when what you're reading is so over the top that you would just love to hear the other celebrity's side of the story.

A good example would be Esther Williams' best-selling memoir from 1999 "The Million Dollar Mermaid" where she claims to have blown the lid off Tinseltown's kinkiest sex secrets, one in particular is where she claims that her former boyfriend, macho movie star heart throb of that era actor Jeff Chandler, was a closeted drag queen?

Well in this case, I kind of have the feeling that she was telling the truth, she hardly seemed like the kind of women that was going to make something like that up to just sell some books (in my opinion). It is well known in Hollywood that after her book came out, most of her Hollywood fellow actor friends would have nothing to do with her ever again!

Unfortunately for Jeff Chandler, he was dead and could not defend himself from her words.

A much more current example would be Kirstie Alley. Now to me, this seems like the kind of women who would make up lies just to sell books. In her book from 2013, she claims that John Travolta was the love of her life and that she and Patrick Swayze fell madly in love with each other while filming a miniseries.

Unfortunately, Patrick was dead and could not respond one way or another to Ms. Alley's words about him... Can you imagine what Patrick would have to say about that if he were alive?

It was no secret who Swayze was in love with, it was his wife Lisa, she was by his side till the end, and in Ms. Alley's own admissions, she cheated one way or another on her husbands and backstabbed two wives of the men she cheated with, so it's really clear the kind of women she's comfortable saying she is, just to sell books, even though those of us in the know, know she is full of BS.

As far as Travolta goes, he was in desperate need of a female to say anything heterosexual about him during his "massage scandal," and I think we're all smart enough to know Travolta was not going to say she was lying.

Patrick & Lisa Swayze had a real marriage. They weren't just married to each other, they completed each other and it was visible to everyone who met them. I mean, is there anybody on the planet that believes Patrick Swayze would choose Kirstie over his beloved Lisa? True love like theirs is only something Kirstie Alley can have on paper after she writes the fiction.

You will never read of men or women coming forward to tell the truth about an affair or a hook up with Swayze, because there were none, he was not Travolta, he really did have it all by Hollywood standards.

It used to be that never would a celebrity even talk truths about each other, and in many cases, they would help to perpetuate the lies of a false Hollywood image, such as Rock Hudson, Ellen DeGeneres or Liberace. It was an unspoken celebrity understanding that went out the window years ago. Now, celebrities write their own tell-alls and tell ALL on their deceased fellow actors. I say "how convenient" and unfair.

I take great pride that I have had the strength and courage to write my two Travolta books... I am doing it while the man is alive, so he can defend himself and tell his side of the story.

Take for example, the modern Hollywood biography, such as "Liberace Behind The Candelabra." Just look how Liberace spent his whole life lying to all his fans and looking for sexual hookups with men, and we now find it interesting enough for grade A stars to play the parts, Michael Douglas and Matt Damon, and after Travolta has passed away, there will be top stars fighting for the chance to play him in his HBO shocker.

"Merv Griffin Inside the Closet"--- I have no doubt it will be made into a movie soon enough. We all knew Merv was gay, but we also knew there would be no talk out in the open while he was alive.

That is why I started "You'll Never Spa In This Town Again" and "Tracking Travolta" with a polygraph, I wanted to show my readers that I was telling the truth and not making up stuff just to sell a book.

With the content of "YNSITTA" never being challenged by Mr. Travolta in any way, shape or form and the fact that he never countersued me for libel says it all.

Addiction can make people do things they would not normally do, I believe this to be the case with Travolta… He is a sex addict and his actions have more than proven that to me.

In all, I was contacted by thousands of people regarding "all things" Travolta and many of them were men who were claiming to be very happy to have hooked up with the star for sex, then there were the ones who had a different story to tell, a story that would break your heart.

Men claiming to me that Travolta had so horribly destroyed their life because they rejected his sex, or that they had accepted his sex and he destroyed them as well. My heart broke for these victims with names like Fabian Zanzi and Chris Williams, to name only a few, telling me they were going to be killing themselves over what they had gone through with Travolta.

I knew I had to try and get these guys some help. I'm sorry to say there are others that I never heard back from, so I'll never know if they went through with what they were telling me they were going to do…"Kill Themselves".

I hope not!!

I originally planned on including many of the stories and people I have met that had so much to share with me about John's wife Kelly Preston, but because of the overwhelming amount of information, I have learned about the fascinating woman, I have decided to write a book about her as well.

There are many paths Ms. Preston crossed on her road to stardom and many of them have deep cracks. I never expected to hear from so many people so close to the actress. When her closest of old friends and family members reached out to me, that's when it really took me in a whole new direction with her, she went from having a chapter in Tracking Travolta to having a whole book dedicated just to her. It's a shocking look into all her secrets, drugs, men, the booze and the truth finally about her first child, and the autism cover up. When I finally heard the truth about what really happened between her and Charlie Sheen and the whole gunshot cover up, I was floored. To really have a grip on the real Kelly Preston is going to knock your socks off!! The book is entitled "Kelly Preston---Unscripted." Coming in the new year...2015

The church of Scientology knew exactly what they were doing when they arranged the marriage between the wannabe actress and the world's biggest movie star. She was a drug addict and a drunk (in her own words), seeking the church's help, and the rest is history.

John and Kelly will go down in movie history as one of the longest running arranged Hollywood couples in show business.

We have all seen the side they have presented to their fans and to the world. I hope you truly enjoy the other side of the Travoltas, the side that was shared with me.

In closing, I want to say: "Keep in mind, it's only Hollywood", and remember there are always three sides to every story. Kick your shoes off and have some fun, I went through death threats and beatings and intimidation tactics of all kinds (that you will read about) to bring this True story to you!!

Welcome to *Tracking Travolta*, separated in sections by the years 2010, 2011, 2012 and 2013.

INTRODUCTION

While writing "YNSITTA" was a freeing experience for me on so many levels, the actual release of my book would come with a great deal of anxiety, and countless sleepless nights. I knew the time would never be right for me, in my mind, so I had to just take the plunge and get the word out there. I made contact with the National Enquirer and TMZ. I had to let somebody finally know I had a book coming out about John Travolta and his secret sex life.

I had gone to great lengths to keep everything quiet up till then. The time was definitely here and I was nervous. Although I had several years to get myself mentally prepared for this time, I still was not. I had many concerns regarding the fallout from my stepping into the spotlight with my book and its stories of Travolta and his dick.

I was no stranger to the allure of fear that surrounded Travolta and his religion, Scientology, and the many tales of woe that came to those who dare speak about any of the church's followers. There were plenty of horror stories out there about what they do to their own members who misbehave, let alone turn their back on the church, Leah Remini, Katie Holmes, Nicole Kidman and Lisa Marie Presley, to name just a few.

So, I had no problem imagining the things they would like to do to me for writing my book about one of their top celebrities, and in time, I would see plenty of death threats come my way.

After all the details were ironed out with the National Enquirer, the first world exclusive cover story ran in September of 2010.

Within days, news of my upcoming book was spreading like wildfire and these men were contacting me. They all had one thing in common---they wanted to get the word out what a sexual deviant John Travolta was, so many of them referred to me as their hero for having the balls to write my book, telling me I was so brave in the face of absolute danger from Travolta and his people, I had no way of knowing it would only be days before I would be chased off the road by thugs and find myself in constant danger and all because I was talking about my book.

After so many emails, it became clear to me that I should put them in a follow up book, these guys were begging me to include their stories in "**YNSITTA**" but that was my story, and I didn't see how I could incorporate them into the book and do them justice, so I decided then and there, that I would help these victims of Travolta's find their voice through me and put out "*Tracking Travolta*". The only change I have made to the emails is I have concealed the senders' personal information for all the obvious reasons, (but make no mistake, I have them at my disposal for witnesses should I need them).

Other than that, you can read for yourself in the words of the victims themselves and see what they had to put up with from the great actor John Travolta. I believe you will find yourself in SHOCK! SHOCK! as I did, and fascinated at the same time. These are the men who know him the best! After you are done reading, I believe you will know Mr. Travolta for who he really is a homosexual sex addict out of control and destroying innocent lives.

I make no apologies for the truths I have written on these pages I have kept the language true to the manner in which it was sent to me, hardcore and vulgar. If this straightforward, honest approach offends you, I suggest you stop here.

If you can handle the truth, I say proceed, knowing I have taken every measure to show you the truth about John Travolta starts here.

For the record, I want to state that I think Mr Travolta is a good actor and a man who has done incredible things with his life , especially considering his education, but that is not going to stop me from writing what I know to be the "Shocking Truth" about a side of the movie star that is beyond deplorable!

I can only hope that in time Mr Travolta will get the help he so desperately needs for his sex addiction, and will stop destroying innocent men's lives all over the world.

TRAVOLTA ENCOUNTER... MARCH 29, 2013 5:45 PICTURES TAKEN

I was sure after my first book came out, the last place I would run into Travolta would be one of the very spas from my book that he and his Attorney violently and vehemently swore he never has been to. Come on now, how stupid could he be? To return to the scene of so much dirty spa sex!

I really was hoping when I named the book "You'll Never Spa In This Town Again" that he wouldn't...wrong!

What's even harder to believe is that I am here once again watching this movie star get his dick sucked. I must say his penis looks enormous, it must be from all the weight loss. He does look much better naked now, but he definitely needs to tone up.

I am positioned in the dry sauna and Travolta truly is a million miles away from my thoughts at this point, but not my physical body, when I look up to see him in the corner getting his dick stroked by this guy.

I truly can't believe he's here again in broad daylight, available to anybody for the price of admission to come in and witness this filthy sex addict's adulterous behaviour!

This is a very sick man, to be back here, doing this. If a cop were to walk in right now, Travolta would be booked for lewd sexually perverted behaviour and sex in an open arena.

I feel as though my heart is going to jump out of my heart at this point. For one, the sauna is hot, and the other is, this is the first time I have encountered him like this again, I never ever in a million years would have thought that he would be giving me my opening chapter for the new book.

But he is and I am going to run with it, a lot has transpired between Travolta and myself since I put out my book YNSITTA, all I can think about doing is getting a picture or calling 911, can you imagine?

"This is 911, what is your emergency?"

"Yes, my emergency is I need a cop to come to this spa to arrest John Travolta, because he is getting his dick sucked in front of me and a bunch of other men"

I'm sure the 911 guys would be laughing it up for a long time about that one!

Back to the scene in front of me…

This guy next to me in the sauna liked what he saw going on between Travolta and that guy, so he starts stroking his dick right there next to me. I want to tell him to stop, but I don't want to get Travolta's attention by freaking this freak out by saying something.

So he's watching John get his dick sucked with me and he is going to town masturbating his own penis as he stares at the action. John guides the guy's other hand or I should say his finger to his butthole, Travolta goes into a spastic seizure of pleasure the minute the guy sticks it in him, right then the freak next to me shots his load (thankfully) and as most men do, he split.

So now I am completely alone, watching Travolta get off, the guy who by the way is a black male with a humongous cock between his legs tries to get Travolta to go down on him, but JT says something to the fact that they should go to the more private upstairs rest area, the guy agrees, and they disappear into the ether.

At this point, I am seriously sick to my stomach from staying in the sauna so long, I watch them leave and I immediately leave the sauna to regain my composure and hydration. I think and think what to do and I do it, of course!

As soon as I was better, I grabbed my phone and headed up there, I had to be very, very quiet… as I got closer to where the guys like to go to get there dick sucked, I heard a very familiar sound, JT getting his cock pleasured, I am just shocked that he is so stupid to be doing this…

I have said it before and I will say it many more times, addiction will take you places you have no business being, and Travolta is absolutely a sex addict and his public display is proof of a man out of control.

I didn't know what to expect when I got up there as far as what Travolta might say or do when he sees me, and I didn't have to wait to find out because right then, the guy says I live around the corner, you can come over... They were now passing me on the stairs, my heart beating in my chest for the obvious reasons, as he approaches, I turn my head to act like I am coughing and they scurry by…

I go undetected, so I thought as I make my way back to the locker room, Travolta is standing there alone while the other guy is getting dressed and John starts berating me, saying, "You certainly don't have any writing skills and that nobody bought your piece of shit book anyway, so who do you think you are anyway?" he says.

I looked right at him and said, "I know who I am and I know who you are too." I threw my clothes on and headed out to my car and sure enough, Mr. Smart Mouth is on my tail with his mouth. He kept saying, "Too bad your dad blew his brains out over your lawsuit against him."

Wow, he was hot with his anger, as I got in my car and he got in his and one point he is right next to me on the street now and he has his window down and is calling me a piece of shit and shaking what I believed at the time to be a gun at me.

I make a U turn and head straight to the Wilshire division police station which is one block away, and at this point Travolta kept on his way, so I felt no urgency to call 911, instead I pulled up to the station and sat there feeling safe and contemplated all that had just taken place between John and myself.

After I gained my composure, I went in and told the desk officer the situation with Travolta, I had to explain that back in 2010 I was run off the road twice by what I believe to be Scientologists and Travolta's people, and that it was all on file with them.

After a while, he came back to me and we went over the situation of what happened in the car again, and at some point he says, "I understand you wrote a book about Travolta and you ran into him just now unexpectedly, and he and you had words and he was shaking something at you. Is it possible that it was a phone that he was on and shaking it and it looked like a gun to you?"

After some thought and the officer telling me that more times than not, people are shaking their phones at someone and it gets mistaken quiet often for a gun in the heat of the moment.

I really was upset when JT was screaming at me and maybe it was his phone, I hated to admit it to myself, but when the officer said that it made me now question if it was a gun or more likely a phone.

I took the officer's advice and did not file an official complaint about what had happened that day, instead, they did what they called an incident report. The more I thought about it, I was glad I listened to the officer because I know as soon as Marty Singer got wind of what went down, he would have said I made the whole thing up, just to get publicity for my book and that his client wasn't even in California on the day in question,

Well I have news for him!

Remember when I told you I grabbed my cell phone to take pictures?

I have 100 % proof that John Travolta was where I said he was and that we had an encounter between us…

A picture is worth a thousand words!

And when needed, I will produce not only these photos, but the photos I have as well of Travolta from Century Spa, as I stated in my first book.

As I drove away from the station, I was wondering, *where did the cute black guy disappear to? The one Travolta was having sex with in the spa earlier?* I don't remember seeing him after John started all his dirty remarks.

I knew, as I drove away from there, JT had given me my first chapter for "**Tracking Travolta**." After all, I'm going to hit him with what I got, and if he doesn't want books about him having sex in spas and pictures of him there being taken, he really should stop going.

Today felt like another episode of the Twilight Zone, with Travolta being back in front of me getting his sex on. The last email I got about Travolta was just a couple of months earlier, I really never thought in a million years I would see him again at one of the spas from my first book "You'll Never Spa In This Town Again." "Hard to believe!" but true.

This is not how I was planning on starting "**Tracking Travolta**." I had no clue or idea that Travolta and I would be crossing paths at a spa again! Especially, with all his constant denial.

So I guess, at this point, since this is a book with e- mails about hooking up with Travolta, I will now start with a very recent 2013 email and then I want to take you back to how it all started.

Though I did not know at the time, the following March 28, 2013 Travolta sexual encounter email happened just twenty four hours before I would run into him in LA on March 29, 2013. The email was sent to me in April of 2013, It wouldn't be noticed that these two Travolta encounters were just twenty four hours apart until later.

What are the odds of that? I guess they are extremely good when you are a out of control sex addict on a mission.

Then I want to take you back to 2010 when I was just a guy who had a book coming out that sounded so hard to believe, and now in the year 2014 the world knows my book "YNSITTA" was true and not fiction or filled with lies.

EMAILS

Here are the emails, retyped for your easy reading. Each red divider marks where each person is writing to me, and the blue divider marks my response. The blue divider also shows where I am writing about what's going on, adding my "two cents."(paperback is B/W sorry) The originals are available to be read at (trackingtravolta.com) and are the original emails, as received from their senders. In most cases the sender's information has been concealed for obvious reasons, in selected cases, it has been left in. I had planned on including the original emails in this book but it drove the production costs up making it impossible to do. Original emails at....https://www.trackingtravolta.com

Subject: John Travolta just sucked me off!!
From: XXXXXXXXXXXXXXXX
Date: March 28, 2013
To: <info@youllneverspainthistownagain.com>

Mr. Randolph, I hope my email gets to you in time to make it into your upcoming book, Tracking Travolta. I'm gonna start by telling you I am a big fan of your work. I admire the way you stand up for yourself and have the strength to go public with the truth.

A friend of mine had told me about the book you wrote called *You'll Never Spa In This Town Again*, so I borrowed it from him and read it this summer. I really liked it and both myself and my buddy knew we were reading the truth. You see many of us gay Orlandians have known for years that John is a closeted homosexual.

The thing is we know this because he has come out of his closet on a lot of occasions and has been a staple at spas thoughout Orlando. That is where I first met John---the Four Seasons spa.

I had seen online that Travolta was cruising for sex at the spa from someone who posted it on craigslist on many occasions, so I went for it and headed to the spa.

Sure enough, I wasn't in there more than 5 minutes when my eyes met John's and we instantly felt a spark.

Within minutes, our spark was shooting all over each other's backs as we took turns fucking each other. He was older, but he was still fun to have sex with LOL

After we both came, we left the spa together, we spoke outside the entrance and he said I hope to see you again. So I said, well why don't I give you my number and he replied, well...I'm married and it would be best not to. I was like, Married? Like he cared about that minutes earlier when he was drinking my cum! I mean who drinks a guy's cum the first time they hook up? So that was it. I hoped we would hook up again, but I never saw any more craigslist ads saying Travolta was there cruising for dick, so I never bothered looking for him again. Spas are not my thing. I only went there to meet him.

Interestingly though, I ran into Travolta Thursday night at Mall at Millenia here in Orlando. It was March 28th, 2013 around 6:30PM. My friend and I were headed to Lucky Brand Jeans in the mall. We were parking our car in parking lot A, when I see Travolta getting out of a van and he's all dressed up and headed to something really classy, I stop my car and say hi to him. Of course, I didn't expect him to remember me. After all, it has been at least three years since we had hooked up at the spa.

Anyway, he acts as if he does remember me and, who knows, maybe he did. He tells me that he is about to go out into the mall to do a store opening for some watch company and if I would like to hang around, he would love to reconnect with me. Wow! I was really impressed that he responded so well to me.

I guess he meant it when he said he would never forget my cock, because he sure seems to remember me. He tells me to come watch the opening and when I see it's over, give him another 45 minutes for him to do a quick interview and wrap up his obligations and then meet him back at his van. My friend was totally blown away! He said he wasn't sure I was telling the truth before about hooking up with Travolta, but now he knew for sure.

We went in the mall and grabbed a Starbucks and watched JT do his thing. The crowd went crazy with his one liners and everyone seemed to be thrilled to be seeing him. I think everyone was surprised that he was there. We had heard nothing about Travolta being in the mall. We just stumbled onto it and so did the rest of the mall's shoppers. My dick was so hard knowing that John and I were about to have sex again.

I told my friend that this time, I want proof of my hook up with John so we planned for him to take pictures of me with Travolta when we met up later for proof. I made sure that I positioned myself behind Travolta when he was doing his opening. You can clearly see me standing right behind him with my big smile. Too bad my hard on didn't make it into the picture ... lol.

After he was done with the show, he caught my eye and let me know he was going to meet me as planned. So I nodded back and headed out to the parking lot to wait for him. He was late. About an hour. I waited, but it was worth the wait.

When he finally showed up, I got in the van with him and we did it. He acted like he hadn't had sex in years. I sat down on the bench seat in the back and he had my pants off me in no time and he immediately started to devour my cock.

I said, hold on... slow down a bit.

He replied, your cum was so good last time, l can't wait for you to nut in my mouth.

I wanted to pleasure him, too, but he said he wanted me to just lay back and let him have his way with me. I obliged. He pulled on my dick, he sucked on my balls, he put fingers up my ass and down my throat... he was on fire! And so was my cock.

I told him I was going to cum and he said give it to me baby, he stuck two fingers up my ass and I shot my load down his throat. He drained every drop of cum out of me. He never touched his own dick and neither did I. And just like that...it was over.

He said he was headed back to LA. He had to be there for Friday. I asked him if I'd ever see him again and he said, I want to make sure I do, and he gave me his number. I could not believe it! I guess I should have known better, because when he drove off, I called the number and it was some out of order number. He could have just been straight with me. He did not have to make me feel like a stupid jerk.

Anyway, you can contact me when you need more information. I most definitely want my story to be included and I am giving you all my contact information, so if you need me to sign anything or ?? , I am available to you.

I really look forward to your upcoming book, Tracking Travolta, and do hope that I find my story included. Keep up the good work. You are an inspiration for gays around the world to stand up for the truth.

My cell XXXXXXX

Work #: xxxxxxxxxxxxx

I hope I hear back from you.

2010

This is the year it all begins for "You'll Never Spa In This Town Again" after spending the previous few years writing the book and putting things together for its eventual release. 2010 would prove to be the year I would get it all together and ready to see the world's reaction to my claims.

With worldwide coverage of the upcoming book, I would find myself facing a whole slew of things I could never have been prepared for. The Internet was giving birth to my book in a way the mainstream media did not. There was interest beyond my wildest dreams. I knew with the focus of my book being John Travolta that I had a pretty good chance of getting a little coverage, what happened next was every writer's dream… The world was talking about Travolta and his sexuality and the claims being made in "You'll Never Spa In This Town Again." This was just the beginning of so many turns and twists on my mission to tell my story.

"Wow! I mean, my feeling about John has always been that we know and we don't care.

Look, I'm sorry that he's uncomfortable with it, and that's all I can say. It only draws more attention to it when you make that kind of legal fuss, just leave it be."

Actress Carrie Fisher 2010

Referring to Travolta's five page letter
to Gawker.com
of lies about me
And he being GAY

From: xxxxxxx
To: robbyrandolph@aol.com
Subject: John Travolta story!
Date: Friday, April 23, 2010, 9:48 AM

Ever since Jett passed, I've been John's secret north of the border lover. Email me back for details, my life has been threatened and I need to know you are for real.

TRACKING TRAVOLTA

From: robbyrandolph@aol.com
To: XXXXXXXX
Subject: Re: John Travolta story!
Date: Friday, April 23, 2010, 3:58 AM

Yes, I'm for real. What do you have to share???

TRACKING TRAVOLTA

From: robbyrandolph@aol.com
To: XXXXXXXX
Subject: Re: John Travolta story!
Date: Thursday, June 17, 2010, 1:34 PM

I THOUGHT YOU HAD SOMETHING TO SAY?????

From: robbyrandolph@aol.com
To: XXXXXXXX
Subject: Re: John Travolta story!
Date: Sunday, July 11, 2010, 9:06 PM

What happened to you????? You went to great lengths to reach me. Did John Travolta kill you? Anyway, I'll be including your email in my book. I'll refer to it as my email from John Travolta's most recent lover. As you said, I'll refer to you as xxxxxxxxxxxx. I hope you don't mind??? Thanks for the extra publicity.

From: xxxxxxx
To: robbyrandolph@aol.com
Subject: Re: John Travolta story!
Date: Friday, July 23, 2010, 11:44 PM

Hello

Sorry Robby! I have been staying off the Internet for a while, due to some really weird things happening.

I am now completely convinced that forces allied with J.T. have been monitoring my activities. So I am writing this from an Internet café. I thought it was time to tell my story...

It all began in February of this year. I am independently wealthy from some software I developed back a few years ago and I like to travel as much as possible.

I was taking in the Olympic experience in Whistler, British Columbia, Canada and decided to have a quiet meal at Il Caminetto di Umberto on the main strip.

I was at the bar ordering a drink, and the bartender and I struck up a conversation about the Georgian luger that had just died on the track. I inquired as to why the restaurant was so empty.

He mentioned that there was a private function in the back, but the celebrity throwing it had decided to open the restaurant to the public at the last minute.

I offered the bartender a "favor" in exchange for entrance into the party, as I had dealings with him before and I always have coke on me.

He escorted me through the kitchen and past a security guard that was an acquaintance of his at the back door. That's when I saw him.

I had always had bisexual leanings, and in my travels, I had been with a few men.

There was a sort of casual confidence around him that said, "Yeah, I'm him."

At the time, I was working out a great deal and I was a little unkempt, so I really stood out.

It was an art show for a friend of JT's, and there were large phallic statues and bizarre African art everywhere. I was quietly admiring the art and drinking my drink, when I was approached by a small man in a dark suit. It was him. He approached me and asked what I thought about the piece we were standing in front of. It was a statue of a small black man with an erection the size of his torso, with his name wrapped around it.

I said that I thought it was a sad commentary on the state of hunger and starvation in Africa. JT said that he felt it was a representation of the Black man's love of their own sexuality and the power they wield through it.

We paced through the small gallery and talked about the pieces we saw there. JT said that he had met the artist, a pale and spindly chain smoker in the corner of the room, at his studio in LA after seeing one of his pieces in a window on Rodeo Dr. He introduced me to Steven Soderbergh, whose work I had admired almost as much as JT's. He invited me to a party back at his rented house higher up in the mountains.

There were about 25 of us, a few of which I had met throughout the night, including Soderbergh, Elvis Costello and his wife Diana Krall.

The house was decorated with the same art as the party was. JT walked me through the pieces in the house, telling me which were his favorites. They were all statues or paintings of naked black men.

I was so star struck upon initially meeting him, that I never thought for a second that he was flirting with me. I couldn't believe that he would actually be into men, so I asked him where Kelly was this weekend, and he quickly said, "Not here!" as he again gripped me by the elbow and started laughing.

We shared a good laugh and made our way back to the rest of the party. Time had really been flying by on our little art tour and many of the guests had left or were otherwise entertained. Elvis and Diana were singing in the main room and everyone but the artist, JT and I were watching.

JT suggested that once most of the guests had left, that the party would move up to the Jacuzzi on the roof and he would be thrilled if I were to stay. I said I would be glad to stay and JT smiled broadly.

I never would have thought that I would ever share a spark with a man of such celebrity, but it was really happening. Once Elvis and Diana's set had finished, everyone seemed to rush out the door and in the flurry of goodbyes, handshakes and kisses, everyone had left. It was just me and him.

The mood suddenly shifted from playful flirting to burning desire, and although the music had stopped, still we danced. No need to get into specifics---I will say that we spent the evening drinking in each other's passion, his fingers and mouth artfully satisfying my wildest dreams.

Weeks later, having left my contact information with JT, I got a text message from a blocked number, "Don't say anything about the Olympics. MDK."

Since I had a job coming up in Seattle, I started noticing strange things: tinted windows, unfamiliar faces, unfriendly eyes.

Initially, I didn't make the connection. That is, until I was in Southern California doing some consulting in Silicon Valley. I began recognizing faces a man at the urinal next to me, a ghost in my rear view mirror. In a moment, like a flash bulb of clarity, I realized those faces, those eyes, belonged to the menagerie of black suits that patrolled the art gallery that cold night in February.

That's when I contacted you… when I had nowhere else to turn.

I must insist you only use my story, not my name. Who knows how far his reach could be. Please do not publish even my assumed name, if you haven't guessed, this isn't my real name. For my safety, please honor my request. I hope to hear back from you.

THE VERY FIRST E- MAIL

You can't imagine how excited I was when I opened my inbox to see this tantalizing message waiting for me. "But how did this guy find me, I wondered? And if he has found me, does Travolta already know about my upcoming plans to release my book "You'll Never Spa In This Town Again"?

After all, I had the web site up and running, but I didn't think without PR that anybody would actually come across it yet, but indeed someone did, and I was fascinated with what he may have to tell me. This would be the beginning of countless emails I would receive in the course of several years, more about those later.

"John's secret north of the border lover" that certainly sounded juicy, I started to wonder if in time I would be hearing from more guys.

I would eventually do the first story with the National Enquirer in five months from this time, and the answer to that question would be yes. I was baited with his opening line and could not wait to hear more. But wait---I would have to wait exactly three months to the day, I finally heard back from him and found the email to be very interesting and sincere and worth the wait. I wondered why he felt Travolta was after him? Simply because they shared a night of passion in the mountains?

I thought if this is what Travolta does to guys he has sex with one time, what will he try to do to me for writing "You'll Never Spa In This Town Again"? I wouldn't have to wait too long for that answer either, in a matter of three months, I would find myself facing the first of many attempts at my life.

I had no way of knowing that this guy was really warning me of things to come and if I had known better, I could have better protected myself from Travolta and his Scientology goons. I, too, would start to notice faces in the crowd that were now more familiar and present.

He contacted me because he said he had nowhere else to turn, I felt compassion for this stranger that shared a bond with me.

"We both knew the real Travolta" and we both knew that if you crossed him the wrong way, he could and would have you killed.

"Don't say anything about the Olympics MDK" we all know that MDK means Murder, Death, Kill. I guess with a message like that you should proceed with extreme caution. I knew that I would have to put my personal fears aside in order for me to go all the way with my upcoming book, so I did. I never heard back from my first emailer that had such a sense of fear in his writing, I can only hope that he is safe and free of any further fear of John Travolta or his people and church.

Subject:
From: xxxxxxxxxx
Date: Thursday, October 7, 2010, 4:50PM

Dear Mr. Randolph:

I want to personally thank you for writing your book. Years ago, when I was married, my husband came home one night from being at the gym and told me that while he was there, he met John Travolta. I'm thinking OMG, John Travolta, no way, right? He went on to tell me that John was gay. I was like, please, how would you know? Then he said, because he tried to have sex with me. I've laughed at him on many occasions, but not as much as at that moment. So I was like, yeah, John Travolta wanted you? He insisted that he did. As usual, we left it at that, with each thinking "whatever."

Years went by and, as life would have it, my husband decided to tell me, after thirteen years of marriage, that he, too, was now GAY. Needless to say, it devastated my life and our children's lives as well. It's been years now and I'm OK with my ex-husband's new life, if you can call it that. Never mind the 13 years he wasted of my life not really wanting me. But wanting to be with men instead. You can't just imagine the betrayal I felt! All those years married to a gay man who didn't want a woman! It took me years of therapy, countless prayers, and the support of my girlfriends to finally put this ordeal behind me.

One day, years later, I asked my ex-husband if he had sex that night at the gym and he said, "YES." It was John Travolta---how could I turn that down? 'Maybe, just maybe, the bastard could have turned it down because he was MARRIED' but he didn't. He went on to tell me the sickening details of how John he's now John all of a sudden, not John Travolta, gave him head and he gave John head as well. He said they exchanged numbers and met up two more times at a bar called the Blue Parrot.

He said they would have a drink, then go to some sleazy motel and have sex. Trying my best not to throw up as he went more into detail telling me how John is a bottom and that he had a boyfriend and that this would be their last time. I'm thinking, why is he telling me this, I could care less, right?

Anyway, he said that he took a picture with John that night. A non-sexual one (who cares) that he eventually showed to me. Let me tell you the shock though still disgusted that came over me when I realized, sure enough, he really was telling the truth.

So the reason I'm so happy your book is coming out is because John's dear wife Kelly is going through the same thing I went through. Let me tell you... I don't know Kelly Preston, but I can't see how any woman deserves to be lied to and cheated on by her husband. A beautiful woman like her could find a straight man to love her (just look at her). No, I'm not bi or Gay, just saying she deserves better.

I'm hoping your book will open her eyes so she can make her own choice to live a life with a man that will truly love her for being a woman. Not a man that's thinking of men when he's lying next to you. (gross) I'm praying that Kelly makes it through all this. Not like me who, in fact, has suffered a nervous breakdown.

John Travolta is the emotional clone of my ex-husband. Selfish and only thinking of himself. At least he should tell her everything, be honest, so she can decide if it's the life she wants to live. Then she will have made her own choice. I had no choice... it was made for me!

Stay strong and remember, the truth is on your side!!!

From: xxxxxxxxxx

To: info@youllneverspainthistownagain.com

Subject: RE: Travolta

Date: Wednesday, September 15, 2010

Hey Robert

John T came into the Summit hotel dining room where I was dining alone and looking good at that time. He paused and glanced at me.

I asked my waiter if that was JT and when he came back to my table, he asked my first name, which I gave, and when he returned with the main course, etc., he brought me an autograph from JT to me.

When JT left, he stopped and glanced at my table, but I froze up as I was nervous… so he left.

The next day, I was having *café au lait* at the café on Robson St. in Vancouver and mentioned to the man at the next table I had seen JT, etc., etc.

He said he was a taxi driver and JT had been his customer the night before and he stopped at gay bars, and had the cabbie wait for him each time, etc. The cab driver said JT has a condo in Vancouver, where he dropped JT off.

He was very open about being gay and cruising gay bars. Vancouver, BC in Canada has an openly gay section like West Hollywood and many gay bars. John's condo was in the West End, where all the gay men and escorts live to service major hotels downtown.

TRACKING TRAVOLTA

From: xxxxxxxxxx
To: info@youllneverspainthistownagain.com
Subject: RE: Travolta
Date: Tuesday, September 14, 2010

I lived in Vancouver in the 90's and my hairdresser at a very upscale salon and I were talking about their doing hair at some movie sets, as I was an extra with Catherine Zeta-Jones, Sylvester Stallone, Burt Reynolds, etc., so we were chatting with stars.

She told me the salon owner had a big party and invited people from the movie set, hoping for more business and Travolta showed up. He took a liking to a young male shampooer, a new employee, but it just happened he was not gay---Travolta seemed to be turned on by the chase and pursued him all evening.

I was in Toronto and John was invited to be interviewed at the show on a TV station on Queen St., I believe. I can get the name of the show still showing out of Toronto) and I happened to be walking by and saw a crowd, so I walked in. John arrived with many bodyguards who were *rumored* to be supplied for him by Scientology and who procure young boys for him. A young teenage boy was standing in front of me and was taken to John and they told him he was the baby in Guess Who's Talking movie. John smiled, said hello and then put his arm around the boy's back and rubbed his ass gently, much to the embarrassment of this young teenager. I was positioned so I could see as could others, no doubt, and I was struck by his recklessness… thought he could caress a teenager in public even (shades of MJ??) at world awards in Monte Carlo with a young boy sitting on his lap, beside Prince Albert, even). I have a bit more info…

TRACKING TRAVOLTA

From: xxxxxxxxxx
To: info@youllneverspainthistownagain.com
Subject: John Travolta
Date: xxxxxxxxx

Great job!

Glad to see the truth about John Travolta in the media. He has been lying to the world forever and he always seems to get away with it. I hope your book, *"You'll Never Spa In This Town Again"* puts an end to his lies once and for all. I'm a gay male, 32 years old, and I met John Travolta in December of 2003 at City Spa.

I had seen him there before, but he never really paid attention to me. On this particular day, he did. He liked what he saw and he made no bones about it. He told me in the steam room that he would love to suck on my cock. I jumped at the chance, even though he looked like shit.

I knew this would be a story I would share for the rest of my life. "The day John Travolta got me off", and get me off he did.

One of the best blow jobs I've ever had!!!!!!

When he finished with me, he sat back and grabbed his dick and said, "What about Johnny?" So I returned the favor. "What a big cock!" If he hadn't made it in legitimate movies, he could have definitely been a porn star with that cock of his.

LOL

Best of luck with the book. How do I get a copy?

Stan xxxxx

From: xxxxxxxxxx

To: info@youllneverspainthistownagain.com

Subject: the Enquirer story

Date: xxxxxxxxx

Robert,

Years ago, I met John Travolta at a little Korean spa "Lyons". He cruised me from the moment I walked in, and followed me everywhere like a little puppy with his tongue hanging out. Just when I was ready to give it up to him, he was gone. Since the place was empty, I left as well. When I got out to the parking lot, there he was, sitting in his white 500 SL and he flagged me over.

When I got over to the car window, I could see he was masturbating. He asked me if I'd like some. I said sure and got in. The parking lot was empty and we jerked each other off. He asked for my number and I gave it to him. He never called, but I'll always have the memory of Travolta in the parking lot. I hope you like my little Travolta story. The day your book comes out, I will be the first person in line to get it. The story in the Enquirer was right on.

Congratulations on a job well done!

From: xxxxxxxxxx

To: info@youllneverspainthistownagain.com

Subject: some hot info

Date: Monday, September 20, 2010 5:44PM

Robert,

My name is xxxxxxx. I worked at City Spa for 8 years. I gave you a lot of massages and John Travolta as well as most other celebs in your book. I have a lot of dirty stories to share with you. Did you ever hear the one about Roberto and Travolta? It's hardcore! Maybe you already know it and it's in your book. Email me back and I'll tell you more. Make sure you are careful and be safe.

TRACKING TRAVOLTA

From: xxxxxxxxxx
To: info@youllneverspainthistownagain.com
Subject: catching up
Date: Monday, September 20, 2010 4:59PM

Robert,

I think I know you from City Spa. My name is Paul. You and I had many conversations over the years about how crazy Travolta carried on right in front of us.

Good for you for writing a book about it all. I had no idea you were attacked at the spa. Although there were rumors going around that someone had been beaten, but I never knew who. Saw the story in the Enquirer... loved it!

Did I ever tell you the time I saw Travolta in the Russian room with Mario? Remember the Latino with the huge dick that everybody wanted? And you claimed to have had??

So, one day, I walk into the Russian room and Mario and Travolta are playing with each other's dicks, as soon as I came in, they left, and I followed them.

They went straight up to the empty massage room upstairs to get it on.

Do you have any stories in the book about Mario?

Give me a call. I would love to catch up with you.

From: xxxxxxxxxx

To: info@youllneverspainthistownagain.com

Subject: Travolta

Date: Monday, September 20, 2010 4:50PM

Hi, you should check out Voda Spa in West Hollywood. I've seen Travolta there many times over the years and he's cruising the guys for sex. "What's the big deal?" Everyone knows he's gay.

A friend of mine worked at Brooks Spa in LA as a masseur and he used to give Travolta massages on a regular basis. He said John always hit him up for sex. It got so bad with John soliciting all the masseurs for sex, that he was eventually banned from the spa. By any chance, is Brooks Spa in your book?

How much does the book cost?

TRACKING TRAVOLTA

From: xxxxxxxxxx
To: info@youllneverspainthistownagain.com
Subject: John Travolta story
Date: Monday, September 20, 2010 6:15PM

I worked at the Hotel Sofitel in West Hollywood from 2005-2007. John Travolta stayed at the hotel several times while I was employed there. It was common knowledge to all the staff that all room service to Mr. Travolta's room was to be from males only and preferably young and cut. The management received a lot of complaints from the room service personnel about Travolta's antics when they would get to the room. One of the servers complained that when he got to Travolta's room to deliver his meal, Travolta only had a robe on, and by the time the server had set up his meal, Travolta had disrobed and came on to the server. Needless to say, the server went straight to management and complained from then on, the management said he could only have female servers. Kinda interesting, huh?

Regards…

From: xxxxxxxxxx
To: robbyrandolph@aol.com
Subject: John Travolta
Date: Monday, October 18, 2010 3:41PM

Robby, my name is Bruce Headrick, author of "Tell Secrets, Tell No Lies". My memoir will be out in April 2011. I was a gay porn star in the 80's and an escort to politicians and the stars. I knew John very well and his lover was my best friend Paul Barressi. They are both in the memoir. If you ever need any legal help or witness or anything, I am here to help and support your book. Please visit my web site www.tellsecretstellnolies.com. I'm in your corner, please get back to me, Bruce Headrick.

TELL SECRETS, TELL NO LIES

From the first email Bruce sent me to the last, he is consistent in every way with his friendship and support of my endeavors. It felt like I knew Bruce for a long time, when in fact we had never met in person, he was a writer who had a book coming out who took the time to reach out to me. From his opening words to his last, he is so generous of spirit and support for a fellow brother on the same path way to the truth.

We would become fast friends and share our daily dilemmas getting our books ready to go to press. It was fun having Bruce in the same shoes as me, another writer who was not afraid to forge ahead with the truth of a life well lived, and he was naming names like me. I was taken aback to how kind Bruce truly was to me in all of our communications to each other. If you were ever in a tight spot and needed someone to really depend on, it would be Bruce. He is a true stand up guy, and he is most definitely "Closetless" his copywritten word.

When his book was finished, I bought it immediately and started reading it. I loved every word on every page, and I was pulled in to his story. Bruce has a true gift for writing and sharing himself with his readers.

His book was exactly what I wanted, my book to be like YNSITTA, all pulled together and it reads so easily. I couldn't help but feel happy for him. I knew it was a real good read and I came away from it feeling like I knew Bruce and his life, and I was touched with his tale.

To name names and then name yourself is a tough thing to do in the business of book writing. It usually comes with lawsuits and books being stopped from being published till they see a judge, but name names he did, and who better to do it than the person who was there.

If writers like Bruce Headrick didn't name names, we would know very little about the stars and their peculiar behaviors and all the juicy sex stuff, too.

So Bruce was best of buddies with Travolta's boyfriend Paul Barressi. It makes perfect sense they were both making pornos at the time in Hollywood. I was touched with his kindness of friendship to a stranger and he would become a great ear to listen to many of my concerns regarding YNSITTA. I would recommend his book to anybody wanting an excellent no holds barred read, "Tell Secrets, Tell No Lies" that's the name of the book. Read it!

We spoke many times over the course of a few years on the phone, what a voice he has, so strong and overpowering in a good way.

You come away with a look into Travolta and Barressi's relationship in Bruce's memoir. As you are transported back to the eighties in LA, the Movie star and the horse-hung porno star, what a combo they made and you can read all about it from the man that was there as their love blossomed.

TRACKING TRAVOLTA

From: xxxxxxxxxx
To: robbyrandolph@aol.com
Subject: Mr. Randolph
Date: Wednesday, October 27, 2010 8:34PM

I am a massage therapist 13 years in Orlando and before that, a concierge at Disney. You can't believe the years JT Smith, aka John Travolta, did to me and why the Ritz Carlton wanted me to do as a ten year employee. I was fired for being 40 years old and they hired a porno star and underwear model to massage him after I had worked on him 8 years at that Ritz property. They fired me and hired a hooker to massage him. I really have no computer skills. If you want info, call me at XXXXXXXX, my number for 32 years. Thanks.

CHRIS WILLIAMS

Chris was the very first person I heard from that wanted to share information about Travolta with me not just by email, but on the phone too. He sent me a couple of emails where he asked me to contact him sooner instead of later. I was nervous about calling him, I wondered, *what info he would have to share?* Although I didn't know the specifics of what he had to tell me, I knew it was covered in sex. I gave Chris a call and we spoke for hours. This would be the start of many men that would contact me through my email to share their personal stories of being with Travolta, with me. I found myself as the "unofficial ambassador to Travolta's secret sex life."

I knew with putting out my book "*You'll Never Spa In This Town Again,*" I was opening up Travolta's closet door, I just had no idea how big his closet was! It's most definitely a walk in!

Chris had such an urgency in his voice when we spoke on the phone as he shared with me the details of his relationship with Travolta, I held onto his every word. He was most definitely drinking and had a real strong sense of a heavy burden with Travolta.

The first thing that Chris said to me was John Travolta has completely ruined my life.

Though this was the first time I would be hearing it from Chris, this was just the beginning of that statement being told to me over and over again.

"John Travolta Ruined My Life"---what a sad thing to hear, and to feel their pain and sense of "helplessness against Travolta" was very hard to get used to, but used to it, I most certainly got, and so will you as you learn the truth about Travolta, and his life through the eyes of the men that know him best, his secret lovers, and sex victims.

Not everyone was a willing participant in Travolta's sex games and most definitely, Chris was not. After his shocking confession of "a life ruined" at the hands of one of the most talented and popular actors of our times, I just listened and let Chris get fifteen years of Travolta off his chest.

Apparently Chris not only had issues with John, but Kelly as well. He flat out said, "she is a fucking bitch!! and "she knows everything Johnny boy is up to".

Chris and John's relationship began as so many relationships begin---with hope, fun, lust and excitement, that is, until Travolta decides years later that Chris is just another burnt out massage therapist that he has used for years and years to get what he wanted from Chris.

Once he dumps Chris for a much younger, better looking masseur, everything in his life unravels and the bottle becomes Chris's confidant and trusted regular. I can hear it in his voice, as he speaks to me the fear of talking about Travolta, along with rage, that from what he tells is very justifiable.

After all, Chris has been working on JTs naked body for over thirteen years at "The Ritz Carlton in Orlando" and though Travolta is not Chris's only celebrity client, he also claims to have been Sylvester Stallone and his wife Jennifer Flavin's masseur, as well as Regis Philbin's.

It is John who has been behaving inappropriately for years with Chris, he says that he has massaged John no less than one hundred times and that every single time John put the moves on him and he claims to have obliged Travolta more times than not.

I can tell from what Chris is saying that he really cared for JT and didn't mind getting him off regularly, because he felt sorry for John that he had few resources to get men other than at the spas or through masseurs, so he said yes over and over again.

I think one of the problems here is that Chris started crushing on Travolta and in the end, it hurt him, when he would learn as I did so many years ago that John Travolta is a male whore and he ain't settling down with no man.

"I can't take one more minute with Travolta and his advances," Chris said on the phone call.

Not only did Chris see to John's every need at the Ritz Carlton, he was also "The Travolta Family" concierge at Walt Disney Hotel Orlando for over ten years…

"Kelly is a lesbian and John is a big fag and they both used me for years and then treated me with disgust for no reason."

He claims that on a regular basis, Kelly would instruct him on making sure Johnny has "A Real Good Rub".

Chris is claiming age discrimination. He says that Travolta had him replaced after he tired of Chris's loyal services, so he was fired and replaced by a super hot underwear model named Paul Anderson who has a web site with a very similar name to it. Chris said, "that Paul is a male whore with a hard body and I have been thrown aside and replaced by this young, beautiful man."

I'd be lying if I didn't say that Chris sounded bitter, but if you went through all he claims to have gone through with Travolta for so many years, I think you would, too.

Apparently, Chris put up with Travolta defecating on the sheets during his massage so many times over the years. He says that John said that he has a hard time keeping his bowels in, because of all the anal sex he has had and he really can't help it when a turd falls out his ass.

Chris says what bothered him most was that John was the worst tipper he had ever seen and since he was getting the movie star off, and cleaning up his shit-stained sheets, he at least felt that Travolta at least owed him a decent tip. I said, "Yeah, right!"

He asked me to hold on while he freshened up his drink…

Absolutely I replied, I wasn't drinking. I wanted to hear every word this guy was sharing with me about Travolta, but I was certainly smoking one cigarette after another during our long phone conversation.

So if I was hearing Chris right, he was a masseur who had been good to not only John but the entire Travolta family, including the overly demanding wife Kelly.

He had practically waited on these people hand and foot for almost fifteen years of his life and he was feeling all used up by them, another common thread I would begin to hear over and over again with every email I would receive.

A web of lies is what we give you at "Disneyland Orlando", said Chris.

"What do you mean by that?" I asked.

Chris said, "Well, it was common procedure when Travolta was staying at the hotel, the management would place an ad on craigslist, acting like they were a single guy remarking on how Travolta was at the spa cruising for sex.

Before you knew it, the spa was flooded with gays looking for John, when John would see a guy he wanted to have sex with, he would tell the "Special Manager" his choice and before you could say 'fuck me please', it was happening to the star.

I asked Chris, "Why did you put up with all of this for so long?"

He said, "I'm a simple guy. I was just doing my job and I always took pride in my job, even when I was breaking the rules and getting Travolta off, but one day I ran into Travolta at the spa on my day off, getting a two hour massage with Paul, my new replacement, "The Underwear Guy".

When I looked into John's eyes, he gave me a look of disgust… a look like I was now trash, and this new young hung thing was replacing me, and sure enough, that day off turned into a permanent thing. I was fired the next day when I showed up to work.

"We don't know what you're talking about, Chris," is all the management could say about his being fired over Travolta wanting him replaced, as if I really thought they would stand up for me. I knew better," he said.

Chris continued, "I had witnessed the hotel break every rule in the book when it came to helping Travolta hook up over the years, so I knew they weren't about to start doing the right thing now, and they didn't, and I was gone.

"With all this time on my hands, I think I will write my own book about my experiences with Travolta."

I could hear the ice hit the glass in his drink as to say fill me up again, and so he did, and I waited again for his return. I was excited to be hearing this kind of information from a complete stranger who had facts and dates and all, about Travolta, what I wasn't expecting was to feel so bad for Chris.

After all, I wrote the book on crushing on Travolta, only to find out you're only a piece of meat to him and he does not care about any part of you except your penis.

I wondered what it was Chris was looking for from me? Maybe just a fellow Travolta person to talk to? I don't know, but I do know I would end up feeling sorry for all the men that would contact me over the course of several years.

When Chris returned, he apologized for talking my ear off, I told him I was happy to listen and to let him get it off his chest. We agreed to talk again another time, and we did, many more times.

The last time I heard from Chris was when Travolta got himself in trouble in April of 2012 with his now famous "Massage Sex Scandal."

He contacted me to tell me how excited he was for me, that the truth was coming out on JT and he was ecstatic that the world was now going to find out what kind of man Travolta really was.

He could not get over the fact that my book had been out for just a couple of months when John went and got himself all wrapped up in a scandal that was basically everything I had just released in February in my book, he asked me, "Do you feel validated?" I laughed and told him I felt validated many years ago.

UPDATE: The following Facebook correspondence between myself and Chris clearly shows this is a man who was at his wit's end!

I am very happy to report Chris did not go through with his plans of killing himself over his situation with Travolta. Instead, he is busy rebuilding the life he says Travolta destroyed. I wish him the best!

TRACKING TRAVOLTA

Chris Williams, Robert Randolph
Robert Randolph Monday, May 14, 2012 at 0:37pm PDT

Chris, it was good to hear from you on my FB page, how are you ??? you have been through so much with Travolta, I'm sorry you went through so much CRAP with him. You have always been so proffessional and you have done everything the way a GOOD person would, I want you to know I'm here for you, These so called Massage therapyst are the very ones that give Massage a bad name. You are the REAL DEAL and John Travolta can NEVER take that away from you!!! Stay strong...Please stay in touch....

Chris Williams Monday, May 14, 2012 at 7:21pm PDT

its bad.......lost job and lawyers involved..........i did nothing wrong but after 7 years lost ritz job because "i could not make client happy" went to hr and lost job

Robert Randolph Monday, May 14, 2012 at 9:54pm PDT

I'm sorry to hear about that...I'm glad you have a Lawyer involved at least you will be protected...I hope he gets you, what you deserve. You know Chris I have spoken to so many people with similar situations, It's really rough out there!!! Stay strong my friend..

Chris Williams Saturday, February 9, 2013 at 4:59pm PST

may 20th is my court date against the ritz carlton spa telling me if i could not make john travolta happy they would hire a 19 year old to pleasure him 3 years waiting on court date..........they have ruined my career.... ▮▮▮▮▮

Robert Randolph Friday, May 3, 2013 at 1:50pm PDT

Hey Chris, how are you doing? I know you were waiting on news for your lawsuit? what happened?? I hope you will get the chance to stand up for yourself after the HORRIBLE way you were treated!! I also hope you are enjoying the day...Take care.

Chris Williams Friday, May 3, 2013 at 3:29pm PDT

Going to mediation. Offered 12 grand. Sad. Cost me my career 10 years with ritz spa !!!

Robert Randolph Monday, May 20, 2013 at 3:56pm PDT

Hey Chris how are you? I think you said today was the day you would know what is up in court, I hope you got the news you deserve....wishing you the best

Chris Williams Monday, May 20, 2013 at 6:26pm PDT

wednesday may 15th we mediated,,,,,,,,,i got pennies........lost 2 jobs.........one ritz carlton spa 9 years.one job loews resort at universal studios orlando 13 years...........both JT lost my job,,,,,,,,,,ive lost everything,,,,,,,my condo of 23 years.my career of 17 years.....no one helped me.........i plan on suicide august when i run out of funds,,my health is bad...lupis.......

TRACKING TRAVOLTA

Robert Randolph Sunday, May 26, 2013 at 4:47pm PDT

Chris, I have been off line for the last week and am just now reading your message....I am so sorry things have gotten so hard on you. I hate to hear you say you plan on killing yourself in August, I don't know how to respond to that, but I do know from looking at your friend list, that you would HURT so many people that love you,and Chris you are so sweet and funny in all you share with everyone on FB I really hope you reconsider...I know in life we ALL have to do what we feel we MUST do!! I just hope you don't!! I want you to know I am not judging your thoughts, I too have had similar thoughts.....John Travolta has caused so MANY people so much hurt and pain. Fabian Zanzi who is the guy I wrote about in my book at the end "The Truth Behind The 2009 Royal Caribbean Enchantment Of The Seas Cruise" also felt like killing himself after Travolta's actions cost him his career. He contacted me and asked for help and I was able to help him. I want to help you too!! I got Fabian my Attorney to represent him and he has settled with Travolta and is also settling with the cruise line. When Fabian contacted me he was sooo depressed and at his witts end and he said he was going to kill himself too. If you can't sue Travolta why don't you write a book about what he did to you?? and how he has destroyed your life? and recoup your losses through that media? Let's put our heads together!! You have a friend in me...Please don't forget that......Again, I'm sorry I just now read your message....Stay strong Chris!

Robert Randolph Friday, September 6, 2013 at 1:01pm PDT

Hi Chris...Glad to see that August has come and gone and you did not KILL yourself!! I hope you stay strong!! even though Travolta shut you down he can't shut me down.....I am sharing your story with the world in my upcoming book "Tracking Travolta" maybe then you will feel better!! Thank you for sharing so much of the lies JT has put out there and all you went through with him and Kelly...(shitty sheets and all) Take care!!

Robert Randolph Friday, September 6, 2013 at 1:02pm PDT
Chris Williams Friday, September 6, 2013 at 1:30pm PDT

definatly include the ritz carlton orlando that covers up and jires young men to please him..........I wish no harm,,,,,,,but i cant work after 17 years as a LMT in orlando......lost 10 year job......... NO COMPLEBSATION.LOST HEALTH CARE.NOW LOSING home.................report the ritz behavior.........mormon owned........

Robert Randolph Friday, September 6, 2013 at 1:47pm PDT

I am going to give them hell......You saw what I did to that back stabbing Travolta.....I will make you PROUD!!! stay in touch....I want the world to know how you were SOOOOO mistreated and then tossed aside.....thanks

TRACKING TRAVOLTA

From: xxxxxxxxxxxx

To: Robbyrandolph robbyrandolph@aol.com

Subject: Chasen Murder

Date: Wednesday, November 24, 2010 4:11PM

Robby:

Please give me a call re: the Chasen murder and possible ties to Travolta and your book. Thanks.

TRACKING TRAVOLTA

Subject: Ronni Chasen Murder

From: info@youllneverspainthistownagain.com

To: gelwell@beverlyhills.org

Date: Monday, December 13, 2010 2:17PM

Detective Elwell:

Earlier in the week, I telephoned the individual who had sent me the emails and left me a contact number.

He said that Ronni Chasen had been John Travolta's publicist for years and that prior to her death, she had leaked out stories about John Travolta to the Hollywood Reporter. He went on to implicate that John Travolta was somehow responsible for the Ronni Chasen murder.

As you can imagine, I found this to be very disturbing.

On Friday, December 10th, I had my personal security go into the Beverly Hills Police Department to pass along the information I received via email. My personal security was given a phone number to Sergeant Mike Publicker, along with two other detectives assigned to the case; Detective Coulter and yourself.

Per our conversation today, I am forwarding you this disconcerting email that I received stating there may possibly be a link between John Travolta, my book "You'll Never Spa In This Town Again," the Ronni Chasen murder, and myself.

I received two emails. One went to info@youllneverspainthistownagain.com and he sent the other one to my personal mail addresses which I will forward to you as well. So expect to receive two emails from me.

THE MURDER OF RONNIE CHASEN

I was watching the evening news when "Breaking News" flashed across the screen.

I watched with interest when they said a very popular publicist has been murdered tonight in Beverly Hills, CA on her way home from a screening of her upcoming movie. The reporter went on to say that Ms. Chasen had possibly been a victim of a hit on her life because this looked like a planned murder.

He described the details that led up to the shooting and I couldn't help but feel so sorry for this woman who came to such a horrible end. The media was splashing this story everywhere and people definitely felt uneasy, especially people in the celebrity circle, there was so much speculation going on with Ms. Chasen's murder.

Can you imagine the shock I felt when I received this email from an attorney that had a story to share with me?

From: Mark Riccardi stuntdble@earthlink.net
To: info@youllneverspainthistownagain.com
Subject: Predator
Date: Friday, October 29, 2010 7:43PM

(STUNTMAN, TRAVOLTA 10 YEAR EMPLOYEE)

Ya know I'm glad to see someone has the balls to come out and show what a predator JT is. I worked with him for 10 years on set and boy, did I see him ruin lives. The only thing that kept me from exposing him was the fact that I was getting paid very well. When he fired me in 2002, I am sure it was because I was too overexposed to his hookups and have seen many things. Anyway, I look forward to your book and I would consider giving you info, but would remain anonymous.

From: Info@youllneverspainthistownagain.com
To: Mark Riccardi stuntdble@earthlink.net
Subject: Predator
Date: Saturday, October 30, 2010 11:15 am

Mark,

I was so surprised by your email. I can't believe all the SHIT you witnessed with Travolta. I would have thought he would have treated you better, especially with all the gay sex you witnessed him having.

I would love to speak with you in person and grab a coffee?

When you called Travolta a predator, I knew you were being totally honest with me... HE IS SUCH A PREDATOR!

John has been lying to all his fans forever... He must really think they are stupid...

My number is xxxxxx. Call me any time.

Again Mark, it was great to hear from you.

Rob

MARK RICCARDI

Exclusive stunt double and coordinator to Travolta

When I heard from Mark, I had no idea who he was but it didn't take me long to know I had hit the jackpot with this email. One of the highlights of Mark's early stunt career was when he began as a stunt double for Jonathan Frakes on Star Trek "The Next Generation." This was the start of a long career for Mark as a stunt man, which eventually led to him working with John Travolta as his exclusive stunt double, stunt coordinator, and 2nd unit director during Travolta's amazing comeback trail.

After all, Mark worked on so many films with Travolta. This was a man who really knew JT and was an employee too, I had penetrated Travolta's deep inner circle.

Up till this point, I was hearing from men who had slept with the star and were either happy with John or not, but this was the first from a *bona fide* ten year employee. To be John Travolta's stunt double is quite a title, with all the credits to show for it, and that is exactly what Mark Riccardi was.

Unfortunately, Mark has been "Travoltanized" into the corn field, more about that in a minute. I was beyond excited to hear what this true Hollywood insider had to say about Travolta.

The first thing Mark said to me was that, I said it best when I called Travolta a predator and that he had witnessed John destroy so many men that he had slept with, Mark was upset and it came through the conversation in his tone of voice.

I came away from our first chat, feeling sorry for Mark for the way Travolta had treated him or better said, not treated him. I truly believe Mark cared for Travolta and was more hurt than anything when he got fired. He felt that Travolta was sick of looking at him, knowing he had so much information on him and was canned.

It was very exciting, listening to Mark describe the scenarios he witnessed with his boss. After all, Mark had been in so many Travolta films: *"Michael"*, *"Get Shorty"*, *"The General's Daughter"*, *"Face Off"*, *"Primary Colors"*, *"Phenomenon"*, *"Swordfish"*, *"A Civil Action"*, *"Broken Arrow"*.

All in all, Mark was in around thirteen Travolta films as his stunt double or his stunt coordinator. He really knew John inside and out. When I first heard from Mark, I Googled him to see if he was the real thing and boy, was I pleasantly surprised to see he was indeed!

When Mark sent me his first unsolicited email about Travolta, he called his boss a predator. He claimed to watch John destroy many men's lives. Here he was again destroying lives, but this time I'm hearing it from this big time stunt double to this big time movie star.

I promised Mark I would not share his second and third, etc. emails to me, and I plan on keeping that promise. I have included the first one he sent me because that's only right, he gave it to me freely with no strings attached.

So we agreed to meet for coffee at Coffee Bean on Sunset Blvd in West Hollywood, I was excited to meet this man who portrays Travolta in a body double way.

Mark is a very good looking man in person, much much better looking in person than Travolta is.

I bet that's why John fired him. When you look at Mark, you feel like you're looking at a good looking version of Travolta, then when you see Travolta, you think 'jeez, he should be the stunt double, not Mark.'

We spotted each other immediately, he commented on my resembling JT and how he couldn't get over what he had seen Travolta do to guys in all the years of working side by side with the star. He told me all about a project he was working on called *"The Mamaluke"* and he was happy with his life away from Travolta, but that he had secretly hoped that JT would someday rehire him.

After all, as Mark said, up till now with you, I have never talked about John and his secret sex life with anyone before. He said he felt compelled to reach out to me and congratulate me for having the balls to stand up to his old boss, the predator.

When he said I said it best when I called Travolta a predator, I knew Mark was being totally open and honest with me. He is definitely straight, but man! if he wasn't, he would certainly be busy with pursuers of the male gender.

You see Mark is the one thing that no matter how hard Travolta tries to act the scene out, he is not straight and it shines through when you watch him, whereas Mark is the straight version of the movie star, so he is really what we all fell in love with in all those Travolta films. The presence of Mark's heterosexuality is what John drew from for all those movies for a decade.

We drank our coffee and talked. We sat there for about an hour. I let Mark get years and years of BS with Travolta off his chest. There were no less than five guys that Mark said he witnessed Travolta destroy after he is done using them for sex.

I used to think of the Mile High Club as a club you joined when you had sex in the air. After hearing what Mark had to say about John up in the air having orgies and getting fucked by numerous men in the back of the plane on their way to some glamorous location, I will never think of it again the same way.

Mark claims Travolta was much more discreet in the early years, but as the years rolled by, John became much looser with his discretion.

Apparently, many things about JT became looser as the years passed. He told me of the gifts Travolta would shower on his love interests, houses, cars, boats, jewelry, you name it! Mark claimed John purchased it for the men of his desires. I found this information to be a sharp contrast to what I had heard all these years about how cheap John was with all the masseurs. I guess John does have a generous side, if you are someone he has a crush on or wants gay sex from.

Besides hearing this information from Mark about all the gifts Travolta showered on these men, I had never heard anything like this.

He also elaborated on Travolta's wife, Kelly Preston, telling me she knew everything about her husband and that she was completely fine with it. After all, he said, she is gay too. "Her and John have a fake marriage set up to fool all his fans."

Mark said on many of the trips they would take in the plane, Kelly always had her girlfriend/assistant with her. He went on to describe Kelly as a pill-popping drunk, and that most of the time when he would see her, she would be in a stupor.

He also said she was an extremely cold woman who had a lot of unresolved issues in her life and they had caught up with her and it was really taking a toll on her. Travolta would often tell Kelly "Just Take A Pill" and walk away from her needs. Her Mothering skills apparently were "nonexistent" and they had nannies to do everything.

"She needs to sober up," he said. Maybe then she would be a better Mother, but until then she is always wasted and hiding behind her substance abuse. He went on to point out to me that when Jett Travolta died in that bathroom in the Bahamas, that poor Jett had been laying there for over thirteen hours alone and dead.

"That is the kind of Mother she was," the kind that could have a son with special needs and she couldn't stay sober long enough to help her child stay alive.

Mark didn't tell me anything about Kelly that I had not already heard many, many times by family members to her, and by past relationships she had with people who reached out to me to share their stories of Ms. Preston and her secrets.

We had been talking for quite some time, when Mark got a call regarding his upcoming new project and he needed to take it, we said our goodbyes and parted.

On my drive home, I thought of all the stories Mark had shared with me about his adventures with the Travoltas and what a great book it would make. I came up with the title *"Confessions Of John Travolta's Stunt Double."* As Mark said, he was thinking of writing his own book about all the years being employed by Travolta and what he went through.

I didn't know it at the time, but that is one book that will never make it to the light of day, due to the fact he was employed by Travolta in one way or another, and as we have seen with Doug Gotterba (the six year boyfriend), if you were employed by Travolta, you are going to be shit out of luck because of the confidentiality agreement.

In December of 2013, Dish Nation did a promo for my upcoming book "Tracking Travolta."

In their piece, they mentioned that Travolta's stunt double had contacted me, and was going to be included in this book when it came out.

Just days later, Mark Riccardi was "Travoltanized" again!

His Twitter account was shut down, and everywhere I looked Mark had been vanished into the corn field by John. His website was gone, all mention of Travolta had already been removed from Mark's life.

Months earlier, when Gawker ran a piece on 4/2/2013 titled "Grease Money Document shows John Travolta's insurance company paid more than 84K to handle sexual assault allegations" and in the piece, Mark's name was mentioned as putting in a demand for money.

From that time on, when I checked out Mark's sites and social media, all mention of John Travolta had been removed.

Once the Dish Nation piece ran later that year and Mark was mentioned, he has now completely vanished from sight in every way connected to Travolta.

When you work for John and you sign an agreement not to talk, you can't, that is what I have learned, good thing I never worked for him. I hope some day Mark Riccardi shows up again in social media, till then though Travolta has shut him up.

John has silenced him, but he can never remove what time has already written regarding Mark Riccardi and John Travolta, and though for now it looks like Travolta has won again and "Wiped Away" a life, he hasn't.

I hope Mark stays strong and has a great life, he is a really nice guy. And I want the world to know what Travolta did to him. I had a lot more I was going to share with you regarding dirty sex stories Mark witnessed and shared with me, but I decided not to. I don't want to add further to the pain Travolta has already brought him.

Since this is a true story, I could not omit Mark from this book, though there was a time when I was still on the fence about it, but when I saw Mark had broken his own silence by putting in the claim for damages that Gawker wrote about, I knew he would understand, since he opened that door.

Now that John has silenced Mark, at least the world can know about it through me, since he will never be able to write about it himself, and who knows, maybe someday I will write "*The Confessions Of John Travolta's Stunt Double.*"

After all, it is juicy and filled with ten years of Travolta's homosexual hookups and lies. Only time will tell.

UPDATE: I am happy to say that Mark is finally back up and running with his social media life, but like I said earlier, he has been "Travoltanized" and all mention of Travolta has been removed from his life and his web site and all media accounts that Mark had, have removed Travolta's name.

From: xxxx
To: info@youllneverspainthistownagain.com
Sent: December, 5, 2010
Subject: Gawker has a letter about you on their site?

Hello Robert Randolph,

I am forwarding you this lovely tidbit I just read this morning on the celebrity web site Gawker, you probably already know about this letter John Travolta's attorney Marty Singer wrote to the site regarding you and your book.

I suggest you have your attorneys reply to Mr. Singer's letter about you. At first glance, it appears to be a letter of intent to Gawker, but after a closer look, it is clear Travolta's people wrote this letter about you to publish worldwide to discredit you. It is a pretty sad attempt at making you look bad, all they say is you are insane! LOL!

I found it very interesting that they could only come up with a weak defense against you.

If you wrote a book of bullshit and lies against Travolta....wouldn't he have sued you for libel?

We are proud of you for standing up for the truth!

xxxxxxxxxxxxxx

TRACKING TRAVOLTA

LAVELY & SINGER
ATTORNEYS AT LAW

November 23, 2010

VIA FACSIMILE: ▓▓▓
& E-MAIL: ▓▓▓

Gaby Darbyshire, Director
GAWKER MEDIA
New York, NY 10012

VIA E-MAIL:
▓▓▓

Remy Stern
Brian Moylan
GAWKER.COM

Re: John Travolta / Robert Randolph, Gawker.com, Gawker Media, et al.
Our File No.: 1027-34

Dear Gaby, Mr. Stern and Mr. Moylan:

We are litigation counsel to John Travolta. We are writing regarding the false and outrageous statements about Mr. Travolta which have been and continue to be published worldwide on the www.gawker.com website (the "Website") in the article entitled "**The Secret Sex Life of John Travolta**" (the "Article").[1] The claims that have been made about Mr. Travolta by so-called author/interior designer Robert Randolph are blatant defamatory lies. Mr. Randolph has stated that he has suffered permanent brain damage, and he has given you and others a bogus story that allegedly occurred prior to his having suffered permanent brain injury. In fact, his stories go back fifteen years, yet inexplicably, he has waited until now to peddle these phony tall tales. If you had undertaken even the most rudimentary investigation prior to posting this story, you would know that Mr. Randolph is a patently unreliable source. Instead, you have published an outrageous, defamatory Attack about Mr. Travolta based on the unfounded and baseless claims of a brain damaged individual who admitted on his own website that he has suffered **permanent brain damage** and has had to re-learn how to "use" his brain. Several people have also reported to our office that Mr. Randolph has been in mental institutions.

Mr. Randolph claims on his own website (www.youlineverpainthistownagain.com), that in October of 2003, he was attacked at City Spa in Los Angeles when another club member "**beat his brains out**" until he was unconscious, bleeding, and near death. Mr. Randolph states "The attack has left me with **permanent brain damage** . . ." He also states that after emerging from a coma, he "went into therapy to learn how to use my brain again." Such a source is

---

[1] The Article currently appears at the URL address
"http://gawker.com/5685811/the-secret-sex-life-of-john-travolta"

Gaby Darbyshire, Remy Stern, Brian Moylan
Re: John Travolta / Robert Randolph, Gawker.com., Gawker Media, et al.
November 23, 2010
Page 2

indisputably unreliable. Relying on someone who suffers from permanent brain damage and needed to re-learn how to "use" his brain – particularly when that source is making extremely defamatory assertions and far-fetched claims -- is reckless in the extreme. Making matters worse, Mr. Randolph's own statements illustrate his animus towards the LA City Spa where he claims many of the incidents in the Article purportedly took place. Mr. Randolph's lack of credibility and propensity and motivation to lie make him unreliable without question. It is telling that admittedly Mr. Randolph has not taken any legal action against the City Spa notwithstanding his claims that his "beloved spa had slammed their doors" on him and subjected him to "life-threatening situations" including by supposedly being "fully aware" that of his alleged attacker's "history of violent outbursts" but doing nothing to warn spa members such as himself.

It is clear that this otherwise unheard-of and supposed "interior designer" and "author" has conjured up sensational, inherently improbable, claims for his own financial gain. Gawker Media is significantly compounding the damages which have already been incurred by my client by repeating Mr. Randolph's preposterous lies on its widely-read website. Publication of the defamatory Article therefore exposes Gawker Media and all those involved in the creation and publication of the Article to substantial liability for defamation, false light invasion of privacy, and commercial misappropriation of my client's name and likeness. Demand is made that you immediately and permanently remove the Article from Gawker's website.

The notion that my client supposedly engaged in multiple adulterous sexual encounters in different public locations in Los Angeles (where he does not live), and that each time, the (nonexistent) events were coincidentally witnessed by your source, is absolutely ridiculous. The contention that my client would engage in adultery in a spa where he could be witnessed by a third party *even once* would be dubious at best. The Article, and Robert Randolph's claims, are elevated to an absurdity by asserting that this supposedly occurred on *multiple* occasions, with several *different* men, and that your source Robert Randolph was supposedly there *each and every time* to personally witness what allegedly occurred and even personally supposedly had an "encounter" with my client.

In the Article, Gawker acknowledges that most media outlets and even **"mainstream tabloids"** are **"skittish about printing"** and are **"too shy to delve into"** Randolph's claims. Mainstream media are undoubtedly "skittish" about re-publishing malicious lies which are based on the say-so of an unreliable and brain-damaged "source" who admittedly has "been busy talking about" his outlandish claims only with disreputable tabloids such as *The National Enquirer* and *Star Magazine*.

Indeed, as further evidence of his unreliability, subsequent to his 2003 attack, Mr. Randolph later peddled lies to the *National Enquirer* about the existence of a "gay sex tape" involving my client at the spa which was allegedly recorded in 2004. This was *after* the 2003

Izaby Darbyshire, Remy Stern, Brian Moylan
Re: **John Travolta / Robert Randolph,** *Gawker.com.*, *Gawker Media*, et al.
November 23, 2010

attack which Mr. Randolph states resulted him permanent brain damage. The brain he had to re-learn to use cannot be relied upon to recall this and other such far-fetched stories. Indeed, Mr. Randolph's credibility is further undermined by his far-fetched and completely absurd account on his website that several months following the attack at City Spa, after he mustered up the courage to return to City Spa, that day the very *same perpetrator* who previously caused him "permanent brain damage" attacked him there for the *second time*. This is particularly far-fetched since Mr. Randolph claims that the identity of the alleged perpetrator was known to law enforcement and they were supposedly searching for him. It is even more far-fetched since he claims that the club owners supposedly permitted the alleged perpetrator to use the club despite knowing that the man was being sought by the police. The utter improbability of this scenario further reveals Mr. Randolph's unreliability as a source.

Not only has Gawker recklessly failed to heed the caution demonstrated by others in the gossip media unwilling to publish the claims of this brain-damaged source with coherently improbable claims, but Gawker has also ignored its source's pronouncements of animosity and hostility motivating his claims. Mr. Randolph's credibility is further undermined by his admission that he has animosity toward City Spa and his motive for writing his alleged "tell-all" is to get even with City Spa. Mr. Randolph admits to this motive on his website:

> My beloved spa had slammed the doors on me and had subjected me to life-threatening situations without so much as a "we're sorry" or anything.
>
> I think more than the beating and the brain damage the way City Spa treated me hurt the most.
>
> It would be years of retraining my brain before I would get the idea for *You'll Never Spa In This Town Again*.
>
> I figure if that's how they treat me, then why can't I treat them the same. I'll share every dirty secret I learned in the 15 years I was a member there.

Thus, Mr. Randolph is admittedly also driven by hostility and a desire for vengeance, in addition to being motivated by financial gain and crippled by brain damage. We cannot imagine a more problematic and unreliable source. The Article falsely asserts lies which are all spun in ridiculously exaggerated, lurid detail by Mr. Randolph, who claims to have actually witnessed my client engaging in the purported "over-the-top kinky" sexual encounters and even been unwillingly subject to an "encounter" with him in the steam room of the spa. These claims — supposedly being made by Randolph in a book he is writing and selling on his website called "You'll Never Spa In This Town Again" — are preposterous, false and defamatory per se. Your source's profit

Gaby Darbyshire, Remy Stern, Brian Moylan
Re: **John Travolta / Robert Randolph**, *Gawker.com*, *Gawker Media*, *et al.*
November 23, 2010
Page 4

motives are obvious. Further, as Gawker itself points out, these supposed "salacious trips to steam rooms" are all the more harmful since "[n]ot only has he been married to Kelly Preston since 1991 (and fathered three children with her, including one that dies and one that's about to be born any day now), he's also a prominent member of the Church of Scientology...."

Your publication of the Article despite numerous indicia demonstrating that Robert Randolph is not a source who is knowledgeable, credible, and may be appropriately relied upon, is extremely reckless. Surely you are aware that Gawker will not be insulated from liability for recklessly parroting defamatory statements supposedly made by this unknown and unreliable individual or in gossip rags such as the *National Enquirer* and *Star Magazine*. By publishing the Article, Gawker is deemed to have adopted Mr. Randolph's defamatory statements, and has incurred liability accordingly. See, e.g., *Khawar v. Globe International, Inc.*, 19 Cal.4th 254, 79 Cal.Rptr.2d 178 (1998) ("one who republishes a defamatory statement is deemed thereby to have adopted it and so may be held liable, together with the person who originated the statement, for resulting injury to the reputation of the defamation victim"); see also, *Jackson v. Paramount Pictures Corp.*, 68 Cal.App.4th 10, 80 Cal.Rptr. 2d 1, 27 (1998) ("when a party repeats a slanderous charge, he is equally guilty of defamation, even though he states the source of the charge and indicates that he is merely repeating a rumor."); Smolla, *Law of Defamation* (2nd Ed. 2004) Vol. 1, §4:91 (secondary publisher, or republisher, may be liable for defamatory publication).

As you know, "[r]epetition of another's words does not release one of responsibility if the repeater knows that the words are false or inherently improbable, or there are obvious reasons to doubt the veracity of the person quoted or the accuracy of his reports...." *Goldwater v. Ginzburg*, 414 F.2d 324, 337 (C.A.N.Y. 1969). It is an enormous understatement to point out that the words of Robert Randolph are inherently improbable. There are exceedingly obvious reasons to doubt his veracity and the accuracy of the information he has supplied. His admitted permanent brain damage, animosity and profit motivation are but a few of the elements making reliance on Mr. Randolph reckless in the extreme.

Based on the foregoing, we demand that you immediately and permanently remove the Article from your website, including from the URL address identified herein and from any and all Gawker-affiliated, website, archives or databases. We also demand publication of an unequivocal and prominent retraction of the false and defamatory statements.

As you know, just this past weekend, Gawker was forced by a Federal Judge to remove a story from its website. You would be well advised to more carefully evaluate the limits of First Amendment protections before thumbing your nose at the foregoing demands.

Please govern yourselves accordingly.

Gaby Darbyshire, Remy Stern, Brian Moylan
Re: John Travolta / Robert Randolph, Gawker.com, Gawker Media, et al.
November 23, 2010

This letter does not constitute a complete or exhaustive statement of all of my client's rights or claims. Nothing stated herein is intended as, nor should it be deemed to constitute, a waiver or relinquishment of any of my client's rights or remedies, whether legal or equitable, all of which are hereby expressly reserved, including with regard to the substantial damages my client has already suffered resulting from Gawker's gross violation of his rights.

Sincerely,

MARTIN D. SINGER

MDS/yeh

cc: Mr. Paul Bloch (via email)
    Ms. Samantha Mast (via email)
    Lynda B. Goldman, Esq.
    Yael E. Holtkamp, Esq.

"Never in my life have I felt so

'VINDICATED'

My Attorney's response letter.

Who BTW, is the greatest man ever!"

LAW OFFICE OF
G. SCOTT SOBEL
8200 WILSHIRE BLVD., SUITE 400
BEVERLY HILLS, CA 90211-2315

GScottSobel@gmail.com

December 15, 2010

BY FACSIMILE & U.S. MAIL:

Martin D. Singer, Esq.
LAVELY & SINGER
2049 Century Park East, Suite 2400
Los Angeles, CA 90067-2906

RE: John Travolta / Robert Randolph / Gawker.com

Dear Mr. Singer:

This office is litigation counsel to Robert Randolph, who seeks corrective action from you with regard to your November 23, 2010 letter to Gawker Media concerning your client, John Travolta.

Your letter is replete with inaccuracies and outright false and defamatory statements. In fact, it would be fair to say that the only parts you got correct are Robert Randolph's name and quotes of his own words.

Yes, Mr. Randolph suffered brain damage in the savage attacks that you seem to deny ever occurred, and he thereafter had to retrain his brain to regain full functionality. The resulting damage was neurological. Thankfully, Mr. Randolph's memory survived perfectly intact. Those attacks are very well substantiated by irrefutable evidence (including police, ambulance, and medical reports), but you chose neither to request evidence nor to investigate – because you know that the attacks occurred.

You misleadingly claim that Mr. Randolph's "phony tall tales" "go back fifteen years," as if they were all ancient history. Yes Mr. Singer, your client's escapades span much more than a couple of decades, and the last contact between Mr. Randolph and Mr. Travolta dates as recently as October 19, 2008 – not exactly ancient history. You complain in your letter that Mr. Randolph "waited until now" to "peddle" his story. In fact, Mr. Randolph initially finished his book in late 2008 and scheduled his publication and press release for January 15, 2009. However, upon the untimely death of Mr. Travolta's son on January 3, 2009, out of consideration for the Travolta family's need to grieve, Mr. Randolph postponed the release and publication for over a year.

Martin D. Singer, Esq.
RE: John Travolta / Robert Randolph / Gawker.com
12/15/10
Page 2

    Moreover, shocking as they may be to you and millions of others, Mr. Travolta's very public behaviors, as witnessed by Mr. Randolph, have been witnessed by many over the decades, and in addition to your client's friend Carrie Fisher, there are many who, if given the chance, will provide eyewitness testimony in support of Mr. Randolph's accurate reports about Mr. Travolta.

    In fact, the truth of each and every statement by Mr. Randolph may be publicly proven in the near future, should your client wish to test the evidence in court. Just give him the chance to prove all of them, and more, in a court of law, because there's plenty of evidence waiting to see the light of day. But we know that Mr. Travolta wouldn't dare, because he knows it's wiser to take his advice from Carrie Fisher than from counsel: Better to simply deny the reports and hide from the truth, than to wage a public legal battle which would prove to the entire world the veracity of Mr. Randolph's reports!

    That aside Mr. Singer, you really crossed the line when you made the false and outrageous, irresponsible and defamatory statement that: *"Several people have also reported to our office that Mr. Randolph has been in mental institutions."* We both know that you will never produce a stitch of credible evidence to support that bald-faced lie, because there is none, because there is absolutely no truth to it. Mr. Randolph has never in his life been in a mental institution.

    Your letter has been published widely in the media. It is obvious that you wrote your letter for public consumption, injecting the false "mental institution" rumor in an attempt to discredit and destroy Mr. Randolph in the public eye. For this, Mr. Singer, you and the client for whom you speak are subject to liability in a court of law. We hereby demand your unequivocal public retraction and apology for the false and defamatory statements made in your letter, including in particular the "mental institution" statement.

    Please govern yourself accordingly.

    This letter does not constitute a complete or exhaustive statement of all of my client's rights or claims. Nothing stated herein is intended as, nor should it be deemed to constitute, a waiver or relinquishment of any of my client's rights or remedies, whether legal or equitable, all of which are hereby expressly reserved, including with regard to the substantial damages my client has already suffered resulting from your gross violation of his rights.

Very sincerely yours,

G. SCOTT SOBEL

GSS/ss

TRACKING TRAVOLTA

From: RemyStern <remy@gawker.com>
To: Robbyrandolph <Robbyrandolph@aol.com>
Subject: Re: Interview - Gawker.com
Date: Mon, Oct 11, 2010 9:54 PM

Hi there,

Tried to reach you earlier today and got your voicemail (or your Stayin' Alive soundtrack, rather!)

I'll try you again tomorrow. Look forward to chatting!

Best,

Remy

TRACKING TRAVOLTA

From: Robbyrandolph <Robbyrandolph@aol.com>
To: remy<remy@gawker.com>
Subject: Re: Interview - Gawker.com
Date: Fri, Oct 8, 2010 11:22 PM

Remy,

Absolutely, on both offers, just let me know what is good for you and I will confirm, sounds like fun. A little inside scoop for you, the tabloids are gonna be putting a lot out there this upcoming week!!!!

Sincerely

Robert Randolph

TRACKING TRAVOLTA

From: Robbyrandolph <Robbyrandolph@aol.com>
To: remy<remy@gawker.com>
Subject: Re: Q&A- Monday
Date: Fri, Oct 15, 2010 5:29 PM

Remy,

I enjoyed speaking with you as well, reach me on my land line. 1:00 PM my time would be great, on Monday. Please confirm and I'll be standing by. Sounds like fun!!!!

Sincerely

Robert Randolph

TRACKING TRAVOLTA

From: Remy Stern
To: robbyrandolph@aol.com
Subject: Re: Marty Singer
Date: Tuesday, December 4, 2010 8:46pm

Thanks for the note, Robby. And thanks for doing the interview – our readers loved it! Glad to hear you're holding strong. We informed Mr. Singer that we do not believe he has a case and we haven't heard from him since. Hope you're enjoying the holiday season.

Best,

Remy

From: Robbyrandolph robbyrandolph@aol.com
To: xxxxxxxxxxxxxx
Subject: Fwd: Marty Singer
Date: Tuesday, December 14, 2010 11:03PM

Dear Remy:

I loved the story you did on me and "You'll Never Spa In This Town Again". I also read the letter Travolta's attorney sent you. It is nothing but lies and my attorney is preparing to file suit against Travolta. Every word in that letter is a total lie and I can prove it (and I will).

John Travolta is a lying hypocrite and I will prove it to the world. Many of his ex-employees are on board with me to bring the truth out, as well as many ex-lovers of his.

Every word you wrote was true!!!!!!!!! And the world will know that very shortly.

Sincerely,

Robert Randolph (written to Remy Stern, www.gawker.com)

THE SECRET SEX LIFE OF JOHN TRAVOLTA

THE LITTLE INTERVIEW THAT WOULD CAUSE A BIG STIR!

I heard from Remy Stern regarding an interview for his web site that he was running at the time, Gawker. I had no idea how influential Gawker was in the world and how many people frequent their site, I do now.

He was such a nice guy from the get-go.

I was hearing from so many people that wanted to interview me that it was a bit overwhelming but very much welcomed, just not anticipated.

I kept missing our appointment on the phone for the interview and in a last ditch effort, he turned the interview over to Brian Moylan who reached me.

I picked up the phone and it was Brian, I had forgotten again, but decided to do it right then and there to just get it over with. I sure would have missed a lot if I had not done that interview---the exclusive interview with me regarding all things sex with Travolta. I really didn't give it another thought after it was done, and moved on with my day.

Brian kept wanting more dirt on JT for the article, so I kept giving and giving and the end result was and is:

"THE SECRET SEX LIFE OF JOHN TRAVOLTA" @ GAWKER.COM.

Travolta would finally break his silence regarding me and my book after seeing this interview. Unfortunately for him, if he had just waited a little bit more, I would have been gone.

JT had gone three months without so much as a mention about me or my book and that is what he should have stuck with, because it was working. Whoever advised him to put out that outlandish five page pack of lies about me should be fired, if they have not been already.

Due to my father's suicide, I really had no desire to go forward any further with the release of my book and more than likely, I would not have. But someone did advise Travolta to state those lies about me, and that was the catalyst for me to come back to life.

My burning desire to prove John Travolta to be a fraud grew through the roof when he attacked me with his lies.

Travolta's attorney would go after Gawker.com, threatening them with a law suit if they did not remove the story. Gawker refused to remove the story and it remains on their site for viewing.

I was proud that inadvertently I gave the interview to the greatest web site ever with real balls to stick with what they know to be the truth.

Subject: I am receiving an error every time I try to pre-order the book on the website

From: xxxxxxx

Date: Tue, Dec 21, 2010 8:45 PM

To: info@youllneverspainthistownagain.com

I hope that it is still being released.

I am sure there are bullies out there trying to keep the truth from being revealed.

Be strong.

Jim

From: xxxxxxxxxxxxx

To: robbyrandolph <robbyrandolph@aol.com>

Subject: you'll never spa in this town again

Date: Sat, Sep 4, 2010 12:05 PM

I am very interested in your book.

I've known of John Travolta's secret life for years.

Where can I buy this book? I am very interested in reading it????

I hope you're not forbidden from publishing this book, as I feel this needs to be known.

I work and help the gay rights movement---but I feel when these loved celebrities are living a lie, they need to be accountable.

my name is xxxxxxxxxxxx. email is xxxxxxxxxx

I am very anxious to read your book. Thank you and thank you for being so brave.

Kathi

Subj:	People magazine
Date:	10/20/2010,10:42:34 PM Pacific Daylight Time
From:	xxxxxxxxxxxxxxx
To:	robbyrandolph@aol.com

I have believed John Travolta to be gay for years. When I tell my girlfriends, they never believe me. I have a question though. How come People magazine or Us or Life and Style won't publish any of this? It is also pretty well known that Hugh Jackman is also gay. Right? Thanks so much. I think it's great what you are doing. I am tired of celebrities lying to the public. I think there might be less homophobia if the public knew some of their beloved stars were homosexual, too.

Anissa

Subject: My belief in you .....

From: mudgie xxxxxxxxxx

Date: Sat, Oct 30, 2010 11:42 AM

To: info@youllneverspainthistownagain.com

I think you're wonderful and brave for doing this. I heard John Travolta was gay for over 20 years. God bless.

M

Subject: book

From: xxxxxxxxxxx

Date: Sun, Sep 19, 2010 9:07 PM

To: info@youllneverspainthistownagain.com

Hello,

I would like one copy of your book. Congratulations on telling your story. You are very brave and I admire that. :)

Cindy

From: info@youllneverspainthistownagain.com
To: Gloria Allred xxxxxxxxxx
Date: 10/17/2010 11:22 PM
Subject: I need HELP!

Dear Ms. Allred, PLEASE HELP ME!! I'm in fear for my life. I believe any day now, I may end up dead. I have a lot to say but little space, so I'll keep it brief and to the point.

I believe John Travolta is trying to have me killed. I was warned he would if I published my book "You'll Never Spa In This Town Again".

I'm being harassed and chased. The police had to escort me home tonight.

I was warned that the church of Scientology would kill me too, if my book came out, and the spa that I wrote about threatened to have the Russian mob that goes to that spa kill me and dump my body with cement at the bottom of a river.

There are police reports on file for all the harassment and deathly car ramming.

I'M COMPLETELY AT MY WIT'S END!!!

I'm fleeing my home as the officers advised me to do.

My book is a true story that I experienced and I have a right to tell my story.

Writing the book about what the spa did to me---it took me from a victim to a survivor, and I need your help, or at least someone you could refer me to.

I have always respected you, for what you stand for. If there's any possibility of having a strong great attorney who is not afraid to tell the truth for her clients---

I'M PRAYING TO GOD IT WOULD BE YOU.

It's very late and I'm trying to get my home packed, so I can go into hiding.

If I don't go through with the book, I'll be the victim again, and I don't want to be the victim again, but I've thought if I just stop and dont go through with my book, what guarantee do I have that they still won't kill me?

I'M PLEADING TO YOU MS. ALLRED, PLEASE HELP ME STAY THE SURVIVOR I'VE BECOME, AND PLEASE HELP ME FIND A WAY TO DO IT WITHOUT JOHN TRAVOLTA KILLING ME TO SHUT ME UP, I HAVE NO WHERE TO TURN, NOWHERE.

IT"S GOTTEN SO SCARY AND WORSE ON A DAILY BASIS, I'M SURE IF I DON'T GET AWAY SOON, I WILL BE DEAD. PLEASE PLEASE, HELP ME.

JOHN TRAVOLTA TOLD ME IF ANYONE EVER TOLD THE TRUTH ABOUT HIS LIFE, THEY WOULD BE KILLED IN AN INSTANT. (AT THIS POINT, I WISH I COULD GO BACK AND NOT DONE THE NATIONAL ENQUIRER STORY TO PROMOTE THE BOOK, BECAUSE NOW I BELIEVE I'VE PROMOTED MY DEATH).

Please think about it, or if you can't, please refer me to someone as strong and powerful as you.

Sincerely,

Robert Randolph Davis

Read disclaimer: yes

Subj: RE: FindLaw FirmSite message from
www.gloriaallred.com
Date: 10/19/2010 10:41:59 AM Pacific Daylight Time
From: XXXXXXXXX
To: robbyrandolph@aol.com

Dear Mr. Davis,

I am in receipt of your email of October 14, 2010. Unfortunately, due to our office's present caseload and upcoming litigation schedule, neither I nor my law firm is in a position to become involved in this matter.

If you desire to pursue further action, I strongly recommend you seek legal counsel immediately to advise you with respect to the statute(s) of limitations and to provide representation without delay.

One source of referral to counsel willing to review matters such as yours is your local County Bar Association.

Neither this office nor any referring lawyer are your lawyers.

We only agreed to review this case and have no obligation to file a lawsuit or claim to protect your rights. No written attorney/client retainer has been entered into.

Our statements are a matter of opinion only and we can make no guarantees. You are free to obtain and solicit other legal advice and we encourage you to do so.

I appreciate your inquiry and wish you success in your pursuit of justice.

Very truly yours,

Gloria Allred
Allred, Maroko & Goldberg
6300 Wilshire Blvd., Ste. 1500
Los Angeles, CA 90048
tel:xxxxxxxxxxxxx
fx: xxxxxxxxxxxxxxx

GLORIA ALLRED

It is really clear to me after revisiting this email I was extremely worried for my safety. At this time in my life on this particular day when I reached out to Ms Allred in such desperation, I had been chased off the road by thugs twice in one day. I'm talking big scary looking thugs.

The first attack on my life on this particular day, 10/7/2010, started in the morning while I was waiting at a red light. This big SUV comes behind me and starts to ram the back end of my car as I am waiting for the light to turn green. I could not pull forward to get away from this nut, because I was facing oncoming high speed traffic while at the light.

So he aggressively keeps pushing my car towards the oncoming cars and a definite accident.

The second I have a chance, I lunge forward into the oncoming traffic and take my chances to get away from this mad man who is trying to kill me by pushing me and my car into the traffic. It was happening so fast, I barely had time to think.

I put the pedal to the medal on my old MBZ and got away with my life.

I would be facing a "repeat performance" against my life in just a couple more hours from a different vehicle and different attacker with all the same charm and charisma as the first psychopath Scientology goons.

Two attacks against your life in one day is a full day of emotional drama on every level.

Was I scared? You bet!

After reporting the attacks with the Wilshire division police department and spending a few hours with the detectives there, and explaining all that was going on in my life at the moment regarding Travolta, the book, and the death threats against my life from the Scientologists, they advised me to go into hiding and that is what I did.

I decided it was important for me to include this email to show just how afraid I was that night, afraid enough to reach out to Gloria Allred for help. She was about as comforting as a bed bug!

I was so green with it all back then. To think Gloria Allred was going to help me when she is already in bed with Marty Singer and has done many private settlements with the man?

It would have been a conflict of interest for her because she clearly is part of the problem. She had already done deals with Singer regarding Travolta, so she could not help me, and I saw nothing to show me that she even cared.

As if she was going to help me? A gay male seeking help from her is not her cup of tea. After all, she is a feminist Lawyer and she stands for female issues. In my hour of desperation, that night with fear, "my female side" must have taken hold of my reasoning when I turned to her for help. I think I was hoping she would make some noise and get these goons to stop what they were doing, trying to kill me.

She was busy with her upcoming TV show "We The People" and had her own things going on, and though I don't hold it against her, I was upset back then, thinking she could have helped me if she wanted to. Then, later, I would learn of the many dealings Allred had with Singer Travolta's attorney over the years and it all made perfect sense.

Conflict of interest!

Gloria Allred doesn't try cases she, "Like Marty Singer" settles most everything that she touches, at all cost avoiding trials. She helps to shovel the shit these celebrities "dump" all over the world, and by doing so, she plays a huge part in deceiving the rest of the world of the truth.

Her client, "John Doe l" was not happy with her performance with his settlement. He continued to reach out to me during that time.

"John Doe 1" wanted to take his lawsuit against Travolta to trial, he told me his number one goal was to show the world what a fraud Travolta was, and he was unhappy with Allred's insistence that he settle and take his money and be happy. He claims he did get a settlement from Travolta through Gloria Allred. How much he did not say and I didn't ask. I knew the going rate for that settlement was probably around eighty thousand dollars, give or take ten or twenty.

Other than the fact that she settles everything and keeps the truth from the public, I have nothing against Ms. Allred. If you're a female and you have a problem with a celebrity, she is still the woman to go see. Hopefully, some day, there will be an attorney who is as well known as Ms Allred for the LGBT community.

2011

I had barely a chance to embrace all the early success "YNSITTA" was getting, including interview requests from all over the world for exclusive stories of the still not released book.

When my father committed suicide, it left me numb with no desire to continue with the release of the book. I was contacted by thousands of people, asking me to please release the book and the truth on Travolta's secret sex life.

I had no idea so many people would be so interested in JT's life like they were, but boy, were they! Diehard fans were writing me, telling me they were dying to get their hands on the book of truths about the star. And then, I would hear from a young man from Chili Conception who would reach out to me (in desperation) to help him with his problems with Travolta's sexual assault against him.

Somehow, I just had to get this innocent man some help, but how? This was John Travolta we were talking about, how was I going to get justice for this victim in a third world country? Time would serve me well with the answers.

"Of course I knew he was gay."

Joan Edwards, Travolta's former assistant 1978-1994

Subject: Sexual harassment by John Travolta in Royal Caribbean International, Enchantment of the Seas

From: Fabian Zanzi
Date: Tuesday, March 8, 2011 3:42PM
To: info@youllneverspainthistownagain.com
Attach: John Travolta.jpg

Good evening,

I'm Fabian Enrique Zanzi Louit. I have been working for 7 years in Royal Caribbean International Cruise Line and I was assigned to take care (on 2009) of the actor John Travolta, ALL HIS ROOM SERVICE REQUESTS.

In the second day, I received sexual harassment from his side and he got naked in front of me. I would like to be in touch with you to publish all the history about John Travolta. If you are interested in this situation, please contact me by this email address and my phone number is xxxxxxxxxxxxxxx.

Please see below the attachment, one of the proved that I have regarding this situation.

Fabian Zanzi

Subject: RE: Lost Email
From: Fabianzanzi@royalcarribeancruise.net
Date: Friday, May 20, 2011 4:41PM
To: randolhp info@youllneverspainthistownagain.com

Thanks for reply. I got your email.

I am in Chile. I resigned Royal Caribbean yesterday. I am at home in Chile and my phone number is xxxxxxxxxxxxxxxx. I have everything on paper work.

My name is Fabian Zanzi Louit.

Let me know I would love to put this history and show people how much you can get affected on your life.

Sincerely…

Subject: Lost Email
To: fabianzanzi@royalcarribeancruise.net
From: info@youllneverspainthistownagain.com
Date: Friday, May 20, 2011 2:29PM

I came across your Email to me just today. I don't know why I am getting it so long after you sent it.

I'm so sorry, I would have gotten right back to you. I found your letter very interesting and would love to talk more. Please let me know that you have received my Email and we can go from there. Again, I truly apologize for this mix-up, I'll wait to hear from you.

Sincerely,

Robert Randolph

FABIAN ZANZI... THE CRUISE SHIP WORKER

I would end up hearing from so many men regarding John Travolta and his sexually abusive ways that it made me sick to my stomach, and I can stomach a lot, compared to most people.

I wrote my book *"You'll Never Spa In This Town Again"* for me, it was a cathartic experience to take my story to the world. I also wrote it for Travolta, the way I see it is, he has lied to the world his whole life about who he is and after years and years of witnessing his illegal sexual conduct in public spas, I had had enough. I did not sign up for this!

One man after another would contact me and tell me their tragic story, it was like a bad dream, but it was no dream---it was reality and I was pulled in to these victim's lives. I kept wondering: is it because he is a Scientologist that he is so abusive to these men while with them? Since his own church condemns homosexuality, is this some kind of Sigmund Freud thing going on in his head? Go out to public spas and expose yourself and your sexual business and then hurt or destroy the men you are with or that you approach? I will never completely know the reasoning behind his behavior, but I will definitely say I have known sex addicts and he is one.

Every story was different and so was every man who contacted me, but no one stood out from the men Travolta abused and sexually molested more than Fabian Zanzi.

He was so innocent and so undeserving of what the movie star put him through.

Fabian made contact with me in January of 2011, five months after the first National Enquirer story came out about my upcoming book. It was a very difficult time in my life, my Father had committed suicide just a couple of months earlier, and I really had no interest in the Travolta stuff that was going on around me. This kid's email was so sad and so hopeless and his life had been destroyed, I just had to find a way to help him.

Making things that much harder would be the fact that Fabian lived in Concepción, Chile. How was I going to be able to help this kid in a third world country? I could not shake the fact that this poor innocent guy was more than likely out of luck and in a terrible way.

I took it one day at a time and focused on trying to give Fabian hope for his future, it was very hard to read his emails and Facebook messages to me and see his life going down the drain and all because he did not have sex with Travolta. I knew I needed time to figure this mess out and come up with a game plan to help fix his broken life.

As time passed, I stayed focused on the upcoming release of "YNSITTA" and continued my support of Fabian. I really had no clue for quite awhile how this was going to progress in a positive way, eventually it would all come to me.

Everything would have been so much easier, if it weren't for the fact that Fabian was in Chile. Just calling him was a nightmare half the time. As our friendship started to grow and he started opening up to me about his life before the Travolta attack, I could see what a wonderful human being this young man was.

He had such a beautiful family that loved him and was there for him during his darkest hour. What started out as a bit of a chore keeping Fabian positive, eventually would turn into a burning desire to see his story told to the world and to have John Travolta held accountable for his actions against this innocent victim.

Fabian comes from a extremely modest life in both worldly possessions and wordly knowledge of things such as the underbelly of dirty Hollywood. He possesses all that matters in this life, truth, integrity, self respect and respect for others and is a very humble and happy person, so to know on a daily basis in our communications between each other that he was losing his will to live as more and more time went by, was a difficult thing to watch. There were more than a few times that I was certain there would be no justice for Fabian, though I dare not let on to him, my mission became keeping him alive and figuring out what I was going to do to save him. It would eventually all come to me, but during this year and a half, it would be very emotionally taxing on me trying to figure this out.

Can you just imagine what I was trying to pull off for this kid?

Holding the great and powerful movie star, with many of the world's dirtiest attorneys in his corner accountable to this victim from a "Third World Country" and let's not forget Travolta's church of Scientology and all their dirty deeds.

But pull it off I did. The fact that you are reading this book should be a hint to you that I am not happy with the end settlement result that Travolta and his people paid out to Fabian. If it had paid the way it should have, I would have been compelled to leave the rest of Fabian's story quiet.

But it didn't, and in the end, Fabian was thrown under the bus by the very Attorney I got him. More about her in a minute. As I said earlier, eventually the game plan to make Travolta pay in all ways for his sexual attack on Fabian would come to me and when it did, I was elated and I knew I would be able to pull it off.

The first thing I knew I needed to do was get him an Attorney to sue Travolta. Now let me tell you when you start asking questions around town about what Attorney will do it, the answer is not many, at least not back then. I don't think suing Travolta comes with the same scare as it used to, but it did back then and it made my task that much harder to do. At the same time, I was getting ready to release my first book "YNSITTA". I got the idea to include a bit of Fabian's story at the end of my book to let Travolta and his people know that they had not gotten away with destroying this young man's life and that the truth was coming to the world soon.

It was titled "The Truth Behind The 2009 Royal Caribbean Enchantment Of The Seas Cruise" and I gave details that I could only have told if it were true, and true it was proven to be by me.

I am very proud of myself for facing Travolta and his herd of mad dog Attorneys, but when it comes to push and shove, I have always stood up for victims and people left with little hope or resources. After all, I had been all of these things, and I understood the desperation of not having a voice to be heard.

Fabian was so excited that I included his introduction in "YNSITTA" and I really felt his spirit coming back to life. Never once did any of Fabians correspondence to me mention getting money from Travolta, he didn't even know that it was a possibility, that is how innocent a person he was.

What mattered to Fabian most was that he wanted to cleanse his soul of what Travolta had done to him and he wanted to warn other innocent future victims that this movie star destroys lives. That was the tone of Fabian's FB and email messages to me.

There have been many turns and twists to this story I am telling you.

When the idea of publishing "Our" correspondences to each other came to me, I was thrilled to think I had found an undeniable look into the truth of what happened and there would be nothing Travolta could twist or say to discredit the truth.

As you read the journals, you will feel Fabian's desperation and pain. You will have no doubt of what really happened to him.

When his settlement was reached and Fabian was going to be given money from Travolta, I did not have any say in the final settlement, though as you will later read, Sarah (our attorney) pleads with me too. I choose for several reasons to slowly distance myself from what was to be the final decision. I did that, mainly because if it didn't go fairly (for Fabian), I would then be free to write my book and tell the truth without feeling bad about it. It did not go fairly for Fabian at all! In the end, he was left with a life destroyed at the hands of John Travolta and his actions. His life was also destroyed by the reckless actions of his attorney, Sarah Golden. The very attorney I trusted to help Fabian, sold him out. When you read what she did to him, you will be left speechless and in complete horror! I do believe in the very beginning Sarah had Fabian's best interest at heart, but after taking several "private " meetings with Travolta's people, Sarah would consciously decide to let Fabian's case sink, and along with it, poor innocent Fabian's life too!

See what happens when an up and coming attorney gets her chance to play in the big leagues with the big boys. Does she do the right thing for her client? Or does she sell him out? See the documented undeniable truth, along with never before seen letters and transcripts of recorded settlement meetings. Read for yourself the truth as it unwinds on a semi-daily basis in two journals. The truth is here! You will be moved to tears for this poor victim as his life comes tumbling down on him after refusing the movie star's sexual advances...

COMING SOON..."TRACKING TRAVOLTA 2" FABIAN'S STORY

Subject: Release Date
From: xxxxxxxxxxx
To: info@youllneverspainthistownagain.com
Date: Sunday, December 19, 2011 10:22 PM

Good morning! I'm dying to read your book "You'll Never Spa In This Town Again." John Travolta being gay is no shock to me. I know two people whose significant others cheated on them with John Travolta. One, a wife of one of the cheaters, actually killed herself. Tragic.

When will your book be released? Hopefully it is still being released?

Thanks,

xxxxxxxx

Subject: John Travolta sighting
From: xxxxxxxxxxx
Date: Tuesday, November 23, 2011 9:54 PM
To: info@youllneverspainthistownagain.com

About 1 ½ years ago, he used to go to Wilshire Spa, another Korean spa. The men's entrance is on Mariposa, just south of Wilshire. It's near the Brass Monkey bar. I don't have a story, didn't see him play. He would go there in the middle of the night, much like he does at Grand Spa. I noticed Wilshire Spa wasn't on your tracking list, so I wanted to let you know. It gets a different group of guys there at night, in addition to the Koreans, homeless guys and/or drug use. And the action is more out of control in the middle of the night than it ever was at Century Spa before their remodel.

I'm not sure though, how writing your book got back at the owners of City Spa? It seems more like you're out to get JT.

Subject: stories I could tell you... oy vey!
From: xxxxxxxxxxx
Date: Monday, September 26, 2011 6:20am
To: info@youllneverspainthistownagain.com

Hello Robert:

I really enjoyed your story in "The National Examiner" and believe every word of it. I am sorry to hear about the awful beating you took, but again, am not the least bit surprised by the attitude City Spa took. I, too, have had "good?" friends abandon me in times of crisis. Good for you for spilling the beans!

You might be interested in some stories I have about certain celebs. I also want to say before I get started that I worked as a stuntman and an extra in Hollywood and Las Vegas and although the movie industry is full to capacity of gay men, gay actors, gay crews, etc., it has to be one of the most homophobic environments I have ever encountered.

Unbelievable!

Everyone is so hypocritical and I have had sexual encounters with guys who then call me the most awful names in front of others. Just assholes!

Anyway---in the 70s, I was at Studio 54 and I saw with my own eyes, John Travolta getting his cock whaled on by a series of guys who lined up to suck him off.

I WATCHED this and so did a bunch of other guests. I couldn't believe it. It was so hot, yet so weird. I was too young and too scared to join in, but did enjoy the peep show.

I know an architect here in Boston and he has done work for Cusack in Chicago several times and has been asked to join in on some very hot and sordid sex orgies with the actor and his "entourage".

He says Cusack can get very kinky with "scat" and golden showers.

I was at the Hollywood Spa in the mid 90's, I think it was and saw Will Smith there.

He was so vocal and forward about it and was coming on to practically every guy there. I know a guy who says he knows for a fact that Will and Tom Cruise are fuck buddies on-the-sly.

Crispin Glover is a longtime queen-o as are Matt Damon and Ben Affleck who I knew when they were students at Cambridge Rindge and Latin here.

I also know several Harvard jocks who swear they did Matt and that he's a total bottom and screams like a girl when you fuck him.

Scott Caan has been out on dates with my friend Al, and Al says Scott told him right out that Alex O'Loughlin is gay, too.

TRACKING TRAVOLTA

Subject: John Travolta gave me an STD
From: xxxxxxxxxxx
Date: November 19, 2010
To: info@youllneverspainthistownagain.com

Hello there!

I came across the story in the Enquirer regarding your book, "You'll Never Spa In This Town Again". I'm glad the truth is finally coming out about John's sexual escapades. I have a short story to share with you.

On July 15, 2006, I went to Century Spa in L.A. to use the facility's steam room and sauna.

I'm a married man and I've always considered myself straight and there has only been one time in my life I have had sex with a man and it was John Travolta.

After disrobing in the locker room I went to take a shower. As soon as I started showering, I noticed this guy staring at me. He wouldn't take his eyes off my dick.

He made me very uncomfortable.

So I hurried up and headed to the steam room where he followed me into. I had no idea who he was.

As I was steaming, he moved closer to me and started talking. It was then I noticed it was John Travolta. He was very overweight and was practically bald. A far cry from the movie star in the movies.

Nonetheless, he started making the moves on me. I was stunned. I told him I was married. And he replied, "So am I." He then laughed and started stroking his dick.

Before I knew it, he had reached over and started stroking mine. I was completely flaccid, in shock, and intrigued all at the same time.

After a minute, I said I was hot and needed to step out. He followed me, we sat on some chairs and cooled down. He was very nice. And he was very into me. Again I was in complete shock thinking, what is John Travolta doing in a place like this.

I got my answer soon… he was looking for dick.

A few minutes later, I returned to the steam room and he followed me in. As we sat there steaming, he again grabbed my dick and I didn't stop him.

Before I knew it, he was giving me a blow job right there in the steam room while stroking his own dick at the same time. As soon as I came, I split.

He asked me for my number and I told him again I'm married. He said I know that. I said I couldn't. I said goodbye and left. A few days later, I noticed some burning when I peed. I went and got checked and sure enough, I had chlamydia.

CAN YOU IMAGINE WHAT WAS GOING THROUGH MY HEAD?

First of all, I couldn't believe I let a guy, John Travolta no less, suck me off. And then to find out he gave me an STD was overwhelming. I guess I was star struck.

What else could it have been? I'm glad the truth is coming out on him. He's a fraud and he gave me an STD.

Please don't use my personal info should you decide to share this email with anyone. But by all means, let me know when that book is released.

Subject: Well done
From: xxxxxxxxxxxxx
Date: Tuesday, September 14, 2011 5:30 PM
To: info@youllneverspainthistownagain.com

I have firsthand knowledge of John Travolta and what I experienced when treating him was something I would like to forget.

Well done on the book

Xxxxxxxxxxxxx

Subject: Century Spa
From: xxxxxxxxxxx
Date: Monday, September 20, 2011 6:22 PM
To: info@youllneverspainthistownagain.com

Mr. Randolph,

I can't wait to read your book. I've been a member at Century Spa for the past ten years. I've witnessed JT getting it on for years and years. I've seen him with a dick in his mouth on more than one occasion. I've even tried to hook up with him, but I hear he is not into Koreans. If only he knew what he was missing, let me tell ya. Can you tell me when your book will be released and if it's going to be available on hardcover or paperback?

By the way, I'm still a member at Century Spa, so please keep this between you and I.

Subject: catching up
From: xxxxxxxxxxx
Date: Monday, September 20, 2011 4:59 PM
To: info@youllneverspainthistownagain.com

Robert

I think I know you from City Spa. My name is Paul. You and I had many conversations over the years about how crazy Travolta carried on right in front of us. Good for you for writing a book about it all. I had no idea you were attacked at the spa. Although there were rumors going around that someone had been beaten, but I never knew who. Saw the story in the Enquirer... loved it! Did I ever tell you the time I saw Travolta in the Russian room with Mario? Remember the Latino with the huge dick that everyone wanted? And you claimed to have had?? So one day, I walk into the Russian room and Mario and Travolta are playing with each other's dicks. As soon as I came in, they left, and I followed them. They went straight up to the empty massage room upstairs to get it on. Do you have any stories in the book about Mario?

Give me a call. I would love to catch up with you.

Subject: City Spa Book
From' xxxxxxx
Date: Thu, Sep 01, 2011 4:54 AM
To: Info@youllneverspainthistownagain.com

Oh my! I have to say, I can't wait to get my hands on your book. I'm not sure I'll be able to stop reading ... wow.

Looking at the page, I see there's a pre-orders link which is non-functional. I NEED TO GET THIS BOOK. LOL.

WILL this book be available as an e-book for Kindle? If not, please make it happen. I can't wait.

Good luck with all your endeavors! I hope and pray you sell billions of books! Xoxoxoxo!

I'm sure that after people read these books, they'll never see these guys the same way again! Good luck!

Subject: When is the book available???

From: xxxxxxxxxxxxxxxx

Date: Wed, Jul 20, 2011 6:03 PM

To: <info@youllneverspainthistownagain.com>

I've been looking forward to your book since I first heard of it last year. When I will it be available to purchase?

I am dying to find out who all is into the "spa experience" at City Spa in Los Angeles!

Who else is in the book besides John Travolta, John Amos, John Cusack, Jeremy Piven, Pauly Shore, George Michael, Jean-Claude Van Damme, Billy Zane, Andy Dick, Paul Giamatti, and more?????

Thank you for your time. I know it will be a huge seller!

Kind Regards,

Marie

Subj: Hi Checking in Worried no updates on site.
Date: 12/20/2011 7:43:34 AM Pacific Standard Time
From: xxxxxxxxxxx
To: Robbyrandolph@aol.com

Hi,

I came across your info and site today and started reading. I find everything very interesting. I think it is crazy that people are being so harsh to you. They take the time out of their day just to email you to talk shit. That's really grown up of them. Anyways, I noticed there haven't been any updates to your site since Oct. Hoping everything is well. I'm not sure this email will even work. Good luck in everything. Hope to hear back.

Jeff

Subject: Re: My Book
From: xxxxxxx
Date: Sat, Mar 03, 2011 11:49 PM
To: <info@youllneverspainthistownagain.com>

Robert,

I never heard from you, so I didn't know if you ever received my message. I just ordered your book from Amazon.com and I will write a review.

You are welcome for my interest. I am sure Travolta put up a fight, but when you are a public person --- that's what happens. I think I mentioned my son-in-law used to work at the Ritz-Carlton in Dana Point and he was very surprised to see Travolta bring a lot of men and young boys into his room. I guess it was the talk of the hotel.

I've always been kind of worried about you putting this book out because not only Travolta is mentioned but if I remember, you were putting other names in the book. I was afraid you might meet with some accident or something. I look forward to reading your book and I wish you well in all your future endeavors.

Sincerely,

Kathi

Subject: Book
From: "Rafterman" xxxxxxxxxx
Date: Mon, Sep 13, 2011 8:57 PM
To: <info@youllneverspainthistownagain.com>

Dear Robert,

Just read about your book in the National Enquirer and I can't wait for it to come out! I am also glad that you survived that attack.

My oldest brother is gay and he was attacked by 6 men and ended up in the hospital with his jaw wired shut, but he survived, Thank God. I'm glad you did too.

I hope you sue!

Anyway, Travolta didn't really shock me, but John Cusack and Paul Giamatti?! OMG!! Please don't tell me Keanu Reeves, Mickey Rourke, or Ron Eldard is in there!

I guess I will have to wait until the book comes out.

I hope it's a bestseller!

Can't wait for all the salacious and shocking details. Good luck in your new life and God Bless...

Sincerely,

Jasmine V. in xxxxxxx

From: info@youllneverspainthistownagain.com
Sent: Tuesday, September 14, 2011 1:14 PM
To: Rafterman
Subject: RE: Book

Jasmine,

What a sweet email, you made my day. Thank you for all your kind heartfelt words. I'm glad your brother survived as well, when the book is closer to the release date, I would love to send you a copy on me, let me know where to send it. It's nice to know there are such sweet people like you!!!!

P.S. I wish you and your brother the best.

Sincerely

Robert Randolph

Subject: RE: Book
From: "Rafterman" xxxxxxxxxxxx
Date: Wed, Sep 15, 2011 7:18 PM
To: <info@youllneverspainthistownagain.com>

Dear Robert,

Thank you so much for replying and offering to send a copy of the book. If you sell it on Amazon, I promise to give it 5 stars and a good review! I hope you make a million! Again, good luck in your new life and maybe this will be the start as a new career as an author, or maybe a gossip columnist, or who knows. I think the sky is the limit! You survived for a reason, just open yourself up to all the possibilities. Always think positive.

There are still good people in this world.

Take good care of yourself.

Love,

Jasmine V

P.S. If your publisher says not to send away free copies, then I'll understand and I won't mind paying full price for it.

From: XXXXXX

To: info@youllneverspainthistownagain.com

Date: October 2, 2011

DEAR SIR:

IF I AM HEARING THIS CORRECTLY, YOU ARE IN A LOT OF DANGER. I HAVE SEEN PEOPLE'S LIVES DESTROYED BY THIS CHURCH. SCIENTOLOGY IS A CULT THAT HAS RUINED LIVES AND MAKE PEOPLE VANISH.

STAY STRONG ROBERT-

MANY OF MY FRIENDS AND I HAVE LEFT THE CHURCH BECAUSE IT BECOMES "CLEAR" IN TIME THAT IT IS ALL ABOUT DRAINING US OF ALL OUR MONEY, ALL IN THE NAME OF A HIGHER CALLING... NOT!!!

IF I CAN ANSWER ANY QUESTIONS FOR YOU, FEEL FREE TO CALL ME.

Subject: RE: Warning
From: xxxxxxxxxxxxx
Date: October 22, 2011
To: info@youllneverspainthistownagain.com

Dear Robert,

Please contact me ASAP. I saw the story in the National Enquirer about your book on Travolta, what a brave man you are to tell your story in the face of sheer danger with the Scientologist personnel...

I want to give you some very helpful advice and pass on some paper work on to you... I was a Scientologist for a very, very long time, I now spend all my time helping other Scientologists get free of the cult.

I am not trying to spook you, from what I read, you have already been ran off the road since your story broke?

Please call me any hour of the day or night... I can help you protect yourself better...

From: xxxxxxxxxxxxx

To: info@youllneverspainthistownagain.com

Sent: November 13, 2011

Subject: RE: Scientology

I have NO DOUBT you are a target for an accident that will not be of your own doing.

These people are not messing around, they mean it!! You being ran off the road was a tease for you... If you can go into hiding and stay out of the public eye for a while, you will be smart to take this advice. I know what I am speaking to you of.

Mr. Randolph, please reach me.

SCIENTOLOGY...

I received many emails from ex-Scientologists, wanting me to be careful and watch my back. I was surprised to hear from so many Scientologists, but when they depart the church, they run.

I knew these people were warning me of things that could come, if I were not careful.

Faith is believing in what you cannot see. Travolta only believes in himself and L. Ron Hubbard. Not God, L. Ron.

Can you imagine when his son Jett died, he was assigned handlers to keep him OK...? For two solid years, he could not be alone with himself or his thoughts... now does this sound like a well rounded human being or a man who has been sheltered from the realities of life?

Two years of babysitting for a full grown man?

It is hard for me to believe there was a time in my life that I wanted to be just like Travolta, I really thought he had it all.

Instead, he is a mess! He can't even process his own son's death with Scientology babysitters to keep him in check?

And, in reality, he was assaulting men all over the globe with his sex drive. He was not at home mourning the loss of Jett. He was ruining the lives of innocent victims, with names like Fabian Zanzi, Chris Williams and many more.

Everybody deals with death differently. Travolta deals with it by having sex in spas for all to see, as detailed in my book, "You'll Never Spa In This Town Again".

What Mr. Travolta left out in his recent interview, where he credits the Scientology handlers that never left his side for two years after Jett's death. Is that they were Right by the movie star's side, as he sexually assaulted all the men that the world has now come to know about.

Destroying innocent men's lives at the drop of a hat!

Travolta's whole existence is so comparable to the children's fable, "The Emperor's New Clothes".

With all his Scientology teaching and self-proclaimed superior status as a human being and the man cannot be left alone for a minute to his own devices?

Does this sound like a person anybody would want to be like?

Instead of Travolta's life representing a life full of love and true family happiness and contentment, it is filled with deception and lies and endless days and nights looking for sex from the next man he meets, an addict does what they have to, to get their drug, and John is no different when it comes to his drug of choice: "Cock!" He can't stop!

And when everybody was telling the Emperor what he wanted to hear about his new clothes, he was so full of himself that he could not see the truth, right in the mirror.

Just like the Emperor in the fable, everyone in Travolta's life, from his attorney, Marty Singer, down to all the vultures at Scientology that hooked John in when he was so young and desperate, lie to him...

Should anybody dare tell MR. Travolta the truth of his life?

They might be cutting their own financial throat, and, by the way, the star has his head so far up his ass like the Emperor, he won't be looking to hear the truth any time soon, if ever...

2012

This is going to be a really memorable year for me and my story. After many postponements of the book's release, it is finally here...

I feel a sense of relief. I have no way of knowing what I am about to go through, just shortly after it hits the market.I hear the news anchor in the background on my TV, saying "Breaking News... John Travolta is being sued by two men, John Doe 1 and John Doe 2, claiming sexual battery."

Within minutes, it was all over the world and my phone and texts and emails were ringing off the hook. Suddenly, mainstream media was calling, and wanted to talk all things Travolta with me.

JT was in hiding, and everybody who couldn't find him contacted me to talk about him and my book.

Men were coming out of the woodwork, making claims of sexual assault and misconduct and most of all, the men were masseurs.

Every other week, it was the Travoltas on the cover of another magazine, with stories about the fallout of their marriage, due to John's secret homosexual life that was no longer secret.

"It's time. ... A movie star like John Travolta come out?!?

"Come on. How many masseurs have to come forward?
Let's do this!"

Actress Rashida Jones 2012

From: Michael Bressler XXXXXXXXXXX
To: robbyrandolph < robbyrandolph@aol.com>
Subject: Fwd: Fabian Zanzi
Date: Mon, Jun 31, 2012 8:16 PM

Dear Mr. Randolph,

Your message below was forwarded to me by xxxxxxx. I am an attorney in Chicago and we represent victims of sexual assault and other torts committed by celebrities. I have also read your book and thought it was very good and very well written. My sincere condolences on the passing of your sweet Mom.

I would like to chat informally and confidentially with you about JT. Please contact me at your earliest convenience.

Regards,

Michael

Michael Bressler, The Bressler Firm LLC Chicago Austin
858 West Armitage Avenue, 150 Chicago, Illinois 60614

Correspondence via iPad

THE ATTORNEY FROM CHICAGO

This is a very interesting man, who kept popping up all over the place. I was hearing his name a lot during the "Massage Scandal". He eventually contacted me and we spoke many times on the phone. He would also go on to talk many times with my and Fabian's attorney, Sarah Golden. Sarah thought it would be a good idea for her and I to meet with Mr. Bressler, since he was wanting to take a meeting (we never did).

I came away from my phone conversations with the man with the feeling he's a great guy. He definitely has his hands in many deals that go on that we never hear about. He was open to assisting and helping anybody that may have reached out to me regarding Travolta.

If I needed help placing these victims with an attorney, Mr. Bressler is so much more than just an attorney, he is a warm-hearted man who really has his client's best interest at heart. I have given his name on several occasions to men who have reached out to me for assistance, whether they contact him or not, I don't know. As I said, he gets things settled and gets them gone, so he may very well have helped the men I referred to him.

From here on in, when I hear from a man in need of help regarding Travolta, it will be Michael Bressler I send them to. He knows how to get things done.

It's a good thing he is secure with his ego, because most of his great work we, the public, never hear about, kind of like the unsung hero.

If I had known of Mr Bressler, I would have contacted him first regarding Fabian Zanzi. I had no idea he existed, had I known, what a difference Fabian's days would be like now, instead of the reality Sarah made happen for poor Fabian.

Mr. Bressler would have demanded and got from Singer all the money his client owed Fabian....You better bet!

There are so many things I would do differently for Fabian if I could go back and do it over, but we all know that isn't possible. What a lovely man he is. In his email to me when he wished me condolences on the passing of my "Sweet" mother, well, he had me there!

UPDATE:

I believe I may have one of Mr. Bressler's clients in my book, Mark Riccardi. It has not been confirmed. I just recently heard this news. It doesn't change my feelings about him, as I said, he handles a lot of things that we never hear about...

On May 11, 2012, at 2:11 PM, OO – OKORIE
OKOROCHA XXXXXXXX wrote:

Is there a Travolta related matter you think I may want to look at?

Thx

Okorie

Kind Regards
Okorie Okorocha
Toxicology/DUI Expert Witness
Nationally Board Certified Trial Lawyer
Email: XXXXXXXXXXXX
Cell – Text – Whatever:

Sent from my iLynx®

From: robbyrandolph < robbyrandolph@aol.com>
To: Okorie Okorocha XXXXXXXXXXXX
Subject: Travolota
Date: xxxxxx

Hello Okorie,

I'm trying to put you in contact with Fabian Zanzi. I have been in contact with him for the last year and a half. I will be speaking to him in a couple of hours. I have all his paper work that supports his case, he sent it to me a long time ago. Also there are a few more victims that I am trying to get to come to you… But they are afraid. I'm sure you have heard that before!!

Sincerely

Author Robert Randolph

OKORIE OKOROCHA

From the moment I saw Mr. Okorocha on the breaking news bulletin, letting the world know John Travolta was being sued by two men for sexual misconduct by the movie star, till now, I am a fan of this man!

His presence was everywhere on those early days of Travolta's "Massage Scandal". I was beyond excited to see this man standing so strong up against Travolta's goons, Singer, Goldman, etc…

He took control of the media and he was telling the world what a pervert Travolta is and he was going to be the man holding the star accountable for his actions in a court of law… Wow! What big balls this Okorocha has to come out like this and take control of the situation.

His mere presence is to behold, and that voice of his! So deep and commanding, I got lost in my thoughts about what this incredible attorney was going to be doing for these victims of Travolta's. To stand up to all, he had to bring his clients' court action to the world. He had to have unbelievable strength, and he did.

This is the kind of attorney you want fighting for you when you need an attorney, he was fearless and it showed as he told reporter after reporter about what Travolta had done to these innocent men. You have no idea how impossibly hard that was to do.

I know how hard that was to do, because that's what I went through when I first started talking about my upcoming book and its content about Travolta. It is like the media was under a "Travolta" spell!?!

Thank God that has passed!

The world has opened up their eyes to all of the actions of John and his sexual problems.

Okorie unfortunately had a client that got dates wrong apparently, and before we knew it, that one case was looking bad and then like things do, a domino effect happened within no time!

This great man was in a compromised position, not of his doing. When the other John Doe got wind of the trouble with the other case, he jumped ship over to Gloria Allred. I believe Gloria had her hand in getting this client the old fashioned way…

When Okorie went after Ms. Allred, I knew he wouldn't get that far.

Unfortunately, Okorie was ambushed all the way around, I am sure he learned a lot during his brush with fame. I hope to see a man like Okorie Okorocha become the male version of Gloria Allred for the gay community. I really wish it would be him.

I had never seen an attorney come out so aggressively to defend a gay victim, regardless of who the perpetrator was, a movie star or just your average Joe.

It was clear to me if Okorie had not had the rug pulled from underneath him, he would have gotten true justice for his clients.

He would have been the man who made Travolta take the stand in the Trial of the Century.

TOOOOO BAD! BUT THERE'S ALWAYS NEXT TIME!

Subject: Hey
From: Israell xxxxxxxxxxxxxx
Date: Mon, Jun 11,2012 2:39 PM
To: "info@youllneverspainthistownagain.com"
<info@youllneverspainthistownagain.com>

I have a very keen, and personal interest in these current John Travolta matters. I noticed how Google recently labeled your site a malware site, I am sure Travolta had nothing to do with it.
Israel

From: info@youllneverspainthistownagain.com
To: Israel. Xxxxxxxxxxxxxxx
Sent: Tuesday, June 12, 2012 12:50 AM
Subject: RE: Hey

Israel,

Hello, thanks for the email. It is pretty clear what happened to my site!!!

But Travolta can't keep me down!!! My site will be back up shortly ...

Subject: Re: Hey
From: Israel xxxxxxxxxxxx
Date: Sat, Jun 23, 2012 2:25 PM
To: "info@youllneverspainthistownagain.com" <info@youllneverspainthistownagain.com>

Let's be friends through this, but I am under confidentiality with my lawsuit, so discretion is KEY!

From: "info@youllneverspainthistownagain.com"
<info@youllneverspainthistownagain.com>
To: Israel xxxxxxxxxxxx
Sent: Saturday, June 23, 2012 4:00 PM
Subject: RE: Hey

Israel,

Hi, I appreciate the support!!!!

Thank you for the encouraging words, I'm not with Allred, because she is a SELL-OUT, I plan on putting JT through hell.

He and Marty have been getting away with sooooooooooooooooo much for sooooooooooo long.

I also had Fabian Zanzi (the cruise ship guy) go through my Attorney with his lawsuit, both suits were filed the same day, his suit should be making the news now.

I can appreciate that you are going through your own STUFF regarding these people. If there is anything I can help you with, just let me know ...

Take care, my friend!!

Robert Randolph

-------- Original Message --------
Subject: Re: Hey
From: Israel xxxxxxxxxxxx
Date: Sat, June 23, 2012 6: 13 am
To: "info@youllneverspainthistownagain.com"

God bless you, I am so proud of you!!!!

When I saw that you filed that lawsuit, you instantly became my hero. I personally know what liars and thieves Travolta and Singer are, and I am the guy who Emailed you to tell you that your website was blacklisted on Google by them. I didn't hear from you, and now I see you made news of the world!!!

Great, don't back down!!!

I think you should also claim the virus and subsequent blacklisting your site got from Google to the press!

I can't reveal who I am because I am involved in a similar matter to yours. However, in time I will.

Israel

From: Israel xxxxxxx
Date: Mon, Jun 25, 2012 7:40 PM
To: info@youllneverspainthistownagain.com

Reading all of the reactions to Fabian's lawsuit made me so happy. God bless you and Fabian for what you are doing, and I hope you will find other victims and get them to come forward. We sadly live in a homophobic world where you and Fabian are thought to be less credible, due to your sexuality.

Travolta is a bully and a creep, and right now my case is laying dormant because I am getting my facts together, but I hope to come out swinging as well pretty soon. Please get other men involved, the public will only believe this when there is enough men involved that the story of old John boy being a victim will be as laughable as his wig.

People should see you and Fabian as heroes, but they need time to shake the "Goody Two-Shoes" image they have of Johnny boy, it will take time but it will happen.

I can wait for you to start using the media to really expose John T.

When I get my facts, and I am clear to support your cause I will, until then I must remain a confidante and friend.

I can tell you that TMZ was ready to pay me 90k for an exclusive interview, you should set up a dignified meeting with them. Of course your lawyer needs to be there, but you are smart enough to make people understand that even both men are gay, consent should be there regardless, does someone have the right to rape someone just because they share the same sexuality, then why is heterosexual rape wrong? And gay rape nothing.

You know Radar and TMZ will publish anything you guys say, make sure your lawyer is OK with it first, but you can get you get so many words to the public right now, you are like a god, this won't last forever, so use your bully pulpit now.

TRACKING TRAVOLTA

Oh lord, I hope the public isn't stupid enough to buy what he is selling ...

http://tv.yahoo.comldaytimeltravolta-son-s-adorable-catchphrase-29873374.html

RELEASE THE OTHER THREE STORIES PLEASE!!!!!! LOL

HI, I AM JOHN TRAVOLTA, MY SON JETT DIED, POOR ME (I am not gay!!!), I MAKE MOTHER'S DAY VIDEOS, ONLY AFTER THE FIRST JOHN DC GAYYYYY!!!!!!!

I KISS MY WIFE IN PUBLIC FOR THE FIRST TIME RIGHT AFTER RANDOLPH AND FABIAN COME FORWARD (I AM NOT FUCK) FUNNY VIDEOS, WHERE THE BUS, I DONT KNOW, OMG, WHAT A FAMILY MAN!!!! (I AM NOT MOTHER FUCKING GAY (((STOP LOOKING F

HAPPY 4th OF' JULY!!!! !

TRACKING TRAVOLTA

Subject: Re: JT and Cruise sharing the spotlight today!!!!
From: Israel xxxxxxxxxxxx
Date: Mon, July 09, 2012 12:52 PM
To: "info@youllneversoainthistownagain,com"

Haven't heard from you in a while, are you still allowed to talk on the down low?

Anyway, Tom Cruise and Katie have reached a quickie divorce settlement, so they spared themselves the media's scrutiny.

Looks like Johnny-boy might be the last man (ahem) standing, or at least something similar to a man.

He tried to beef up his career with The Savage's premier, and the movie is a flop, oh well, in two weeks it will be on Pay Per View.

Travolta is just one event away from another perfect storm.

TRACKING TRAVOLTA

-------- Original Message --------
Subject: Re: Hey buddy!!
From: Israel xxxxxxx
Date: Thu, July 12, 2012 1:08 PM
To: "info@youllneverspainthistownaqain.com"

OK, it's Thursday, did your leads pan out?? My project is coming along sweetly. Trust me, the time is now!

Subject: Re: Hey buddy
From: Israel xxxxxxxxxxxx
Date: Fri, Jul13, 2012 7:43 am
To: info@youllneverspainthistownagain.com

Would your attorney be interested JD#1 with evidence that no one knows about, I would be up for confidential meeting!!!

STRICTLY CONFIDENTIAL... !!!!!

But, you are a brother in the same cause.

Let me know, and do not tell anyone, Allred would blow a gasket!

Subject: Travolta
From: Israel xxxxxxxxxxxxx
Date: Sat, July 28, 2012 9:09 PM
To: "info@youllneverspainthistownagain.com"

Robert:

We have talked long before all these lawsuits and adventures, so I humbly request that we take our friendship to the next level.

Before I sign up with your guy, I need a little more info. Are you guys actually getting Singer to settle or is this war just starting?

I know you're under a confidentiality agreement, but I would like to know what I joining up with. Are you and Fabian settled, or is this crap still up in the air.

Just send me a separate email not attached to anything with just an 's' for settled or 'u' for up in the air. Then I would know a little to make my next decision and I doubt an 's' or 'u' in an email by itself is evidence of anything, but I will know.

Respect

TRACKING TRAVOLTA

Subject: RE: Travolta
From: info@youllneverspainthistownagain.com
Date: Sun, Jul 29, 2012 5:55 PM
To: Israel xxxxxxxxx

As I stated before, if you need some assistance with an issue regarding John Travolta, I have a very good Attorney that can assist you. Please understand that until you let me in on your secret!! I really can't be revealing any more information to you...

You made many claims in your email to me that are not correct.

Israel,

If you need some help, I can pass your information on, if not, I understand.

Sincerely
Robert

Subject: Re: Travolta
From: Israel xxxxxxxxxxxxx
Date: Sun, Jul 29, 2012 8:42 PM
To: "<info@youllneverspainthistownagain.com>"

You have been more than fair. We are both bound by confidentiality agreements with our respective attorneys. So I guess we need to chill for now, since neither one of us can let our respective cats out of the bag.

-------- Original Message --------
Subject: Re: Travolta
From: Israel xxxxxxxxxxxxx
Date: Fri, July 27, 2012 2: 18 PM
To: <info@youllneverspainthistownagain.com>

Is yours holding up against Singer?

Sent from my iPhone

From: <info@youllneverspainthistownagain.com>

Yes, it is & if you need help making yours hold up against that LOSER, Singer, and Travolta, let me know.

I'm helping six other guys at the moment figure out what direction to go in... remember, there are more than one way to skin a cat!! LOL!

Don't let those BIG FAT LOSERS get you down.

Remember, they have been getting away with whatever they want for years now, that is before Robert Randolph got the whole ball rolling in September 2010, and I don't plan on stopping until the TRUTH is 100% clear to EVERYONE.

So one way or another, my brother, TRUST ME, you will be vindicated!!!!!

I'm here for you!!!!

Robert

Subject: Re: We are kicking Travolta & Singer's Ass, with the TRUTH!!!
From: Israel xxxxxxxxx
Date: Fri, Jul 27, 2012 7:05 PM
To: <info@youllneverspainthistownagain.com>

Ok, but are you planning on court battles or negotiating with them? I won't repeat anything to anyone we have talked before you even got into the lawsuit deal, and I never said a word. Six more, Jesus, you told me last time it was three.

How has negotiations with Singer gone so far, there is like nothing in the press, I assumed you and Fabian settled, I thought I was alone.

Ok, are the cases still out there, and when is the other six going to hit the press?

To: < info@youllneverspainthistownagain.com>

What's cooking, how is your case coming?

And Fabian?

Sent from my iPad

<info@youllneverspainthistownagain.com> wrote:

Everything is VERY positive on my end!!! I get the feeling the same is true for you as well.

I wanted to say hi, I'm having a great summer!!!!

Take care. ....

Subject: Re: Travolta
From: Israel xxxxxxxxxxxxxx
Date: Fri, July 27, 2012 5:30 am
To: <info@youllneverspainthistownagain.com>

It's cool, I guess you guys are negotiating, can you at least say that.

JOHN DOE 1....

This guy was on a vengeance to get Travolta---he kept emailing me asking me questions regarding Travolta's dick size and other identifying marks on his body that he might have.

I knew from the get-go this man was after Travolta and wanting details to sue him or ?

I don't need to buy into the hype with these true victims of Travolta's unwanted sex advances and assaults because they are real victims, but I have no patience for somebody making a claim against Travolta through me that I feel is false. Here's the thing---if he was really with Travolta and the sexual assault took place as he claimed, there would be no need to ask me what Travolta's dick size was, right?

I replied to his several requests by telling him he would have to wait and buy my book YNSITTA and read it for himself to find out those details that I had mentioned about the movie star's body parts.

After my book was released, he found his way to resurface with his claims about Travolta and his incident with his dick size in place for the legal brief. He then goes on to do a deal with the National Enquirer and tell his story. And what a tale it was! "I loved it!"

The whole alleged attack and bad behavior took place at my second all time favorite hotel, "The Beverly Hills Hotel" and from the description of the bungalow, it sounds like it was my favorite one, having stayed there many times over the years. The Polo Lounge was really something in its day, still a nice place to visit but when I went there on a regular basis, it was the place. Now I boycott the hotel!

So his story in the National Enquirer was great and I waited to see what was going to come of it---didn't take long to see. This so-called "John Doe 1" who didn't put his face to his made-up story was emailing me on a regular basis, trying to get more information about John from me. I didn't give him shit.

Anybody that is going to try and be a man and stand up for themselves and sue someone over such heavy duty claims, and then doesn't have the guts to put his name and face behind it is no man, he's a fraud, and I knew it from the start.

Who gets the date wrong of your supposed horrific sexual attack from the movie star? If you can't have your facts and dates straight when you're making claims about Travolta, you better know you are going to be exposed--- if it's proven that Travolta was on another coast on the date of your alleged attack.

That pretty much said it all. I do believe something happened between those two, John Travolta and this "John Doe 1", but what really happened I think was a masseur who met Travolta and decided to concoct a story.

I am not saying that every bit of his story sounded true to me at first, but with his constant contact with me trying to learn facts and information on the lawsuits I had going against Travolta, mine and Fabian Zanzi's, I could read between the lines.

I included his emails that you have read, as you see he clearly states that he is "John Doe 1", and he goes on to state that TMZ was going to pay him 90k for an interview? I know for a fact that TMZ does pay for stories, because they used me to find Fabian Zanzi when the" massage scandal" was at its peak and when they located him, they did pay him to talk, but he was only paid $1,000.00.

Can you imagine? At that moment in time, Fabian Zanzi, the cruise ship worker Travolta assaulted, was the most sought out interview in the world just behind Travolta himself and he was in hiding. I had secured for Fabian $50,000 for a magazine exclusive interview, but TMZ beat me to the punch by tricking me with their employee, Morgan, that I had talked with on several occasions during the whole Travolta scandal and though she is a sweet girl, she pulled a fast one on me when she called.

I told her exactly where Fabian was hiding and TMZ sent one of their foreign correspondents to meet with Fabian and get him to talk. I have learned all is fair in love and war and getting the story first!

I do believe that "John Doe 1" was really close to pulling his scam on Travolta, but when you can't get your date straight, what can anybody believe that he said?

He stated several times during our correspondences that he was under a confidentiality clause and could not talk legally, but could sneak behind the system and reach out to me for information. Doesn't that say it all about this "John Doe 1"?

When Okorie Okorocha, the attorney for "John Doe 1" found out his client's facts were wrong, I felt bad for him because that is an attorney I would want fighting for me, too bad his client was less than truthful.

In order for these victim's stories and emails to be in my book, they had to be willing to prove to me in many ways that they were telling the truth regarding their assault or attack from JT.

First and foremost, they had to be willing to tell their names and give me all their personal information so if needed, they could be called to testify to what they had shared with me, I was not going to be filling a book with stories from men that were not true.

If you're going to make claims to me about John Travolta and what he did to you and you want me to help you tell your story for the right reasons, I am open to that. I went above and beyond to make sure the stories I have shared with you have really happened.

I have no information on "John Doe 2", except for the information we all now know since Gloria Allred got him his settlement. I believe as well that Ms. Gloria Allred got a settlement for "John Doe 1." As he stated many times in his emails, it was working itself out.

"John Doe 2" never sent me an email as far as I could tell. Keep in mind, many guys would contact me for information on JT to use against him, and when they would do so, they would use an alias with me.

Unless they were willing to give me upfront their personal information for me to check them out, they did not make it into this book.

For the most part, I heard from true victims of Travolta's unwanted advances and when they told me they had nowhere else to turn, well I knew I had to help them. So help them I hope I have done by sharing their stories that they wanted told.

But in the case of this "John Doe 1", I have little patience for someone I do not believe to be telling "the Whole Truth" and especially being a coward and not showing your face or stating your name?

MY BOOK RELEASE---FEBRUARY 18, 2012---JT'S BIRTHDAY

I finally released my book "YNSITTA" on Travolta's birthday, not as a premeditated thing. It was just a fluke, I have a hard time remembering my best friend's birthday, let alone Travolta's.

In May of 2012, three months later, Travolta found himself being sued by two men, "John Doe 1" and "John Doe 2". He was in the beginning stages of a full blown sex scandal.

I was repeatedly asked to give interviews regarding Travolta, because I was planning on filing my own lawsuit against him and Marty Singer. I choose not to speak to the media, instead looking forward to my day in court. I felt that if I was to be taken serious with my lawsuit, I should wait to talk.

It was a writer's dream come true to find their book at the forefront of a scandal that was taking the world by storm, and I choose to turn every offer down... That was dumb!

Again, I was planning on my law suit against Travolta and I did not want to cash in on the offers to talk about YNSITTA, thinking it would look bad in court.

In the end, I was foolish to think my lawsuit was going to hold up with the star-struck judge I had. He adores celebrities, and the first thing my attorney should have done is to have gotten my case heard elsewhere...

Big mistake on my attorney's part, and mine too, now that I know how it really goes down in Hollywood.

It had been almost two years since the first National Enquirer story came out. "You'll Never Spa In This Town Again" was way past its original release date.

Shortly after the first story came out, a month later, my father committed suicide. It traumatized me to the state of not caring whether I released the book or not.

I got a phone call from my attorney who was trying to figure out which Robert Davis had killed himself, my father or me. At the time of my father's suicide, we were estranged, to say the least. I had a lawsuit going against my father and my two brothers for their treatment of my mother leading up to her death. It was a wrongful death lawsuit.

Making the decision to file such a lawsuit against my family was one of the hardest things I have ever done in my life, and I would do it again in a second.

My father murdered my mother by fatally injecting her with morphine that he had stockpiled up during her illness from cancer. At the same time, he had been having an affair with a woman for three years, while my mother lay bedridden and dying at home.

My two brothers were listed as caregivers to my mother during this time, and since they had witnessed my father's adulterous behavior and neglect of my mother and did nothing to protect our mom, I included them in the lawsuit like I should have.

My mother was an incredible woman and she was loved by everybody that met her and she deserved much better than what my family gave her in her final years, so I took action with the courts to hold them accountable for what they did to my mom, and she would have done the same thing for me.

So when my dad choose to kill himself in November of 2010, it was a very sad and shocking thing to be a part of, for many more reasons than just the few I shared with you.

Suicide is very hard to deal with, but deal with it I did.

I pretty much went into full blown depression and shut the world out while I mourned the tragic death of a man I loved all my life, my father. And though I would spend most of my life never feeling the love returned to me by my dad, it did not deflect from my adoration for him and my longing for his love.

So while I ate my way through my depression and put on thirty pounds of fat, my book sat on the back burner of importance in my life.

There had been so many stories written about YNSITTA all around the world in every language and on every celebrity web site that I had already felt the sense of vindication that I probably would have gotten if I had released it on time.

I had to get back on with my life. At this point, my dad was now deceased for a year and a half and I could do no more mourning or weight gain, so I pushed with all I had to resurrect my life from the despair of suicide and depression.

Now the funny thing was at this point I didn't care anymore about putting the book out, but I did for all the people who had contacted me with their support and love and anticipation of the YNSITTA release. I also knew, more than anything, I had to go through with it for all the young LGBTs in the world that need to know that Travolta is gay and that even though he is not telling it to help or inspire our youth because he is a fraud and a homosexual hypocrite, I could and would do it for him!

So for those reasons and those reasons alone I went through with the release of "You'll Never Spa In This Town Again" and have never looked back.

CARRIE FISHER

When anticipating the fall out that might come from my upcoming book, YNSITTA, I wondered how many, if any, celebrities might speak up for Travolta in his defense against the claims in my book.

I didn't even dare dream that it would go the other way for the movie star. Instead of defending Travolta, his peers outed him for the truth of the life they had witnessed as a lie, and in the same vein of my book.

Carrie Fisher was and is my hero!

She not only had the balls to say it the way it is with Travolta, she gave him some very good advice.

"WOW, I mean my feeling about John has always been that we know and we don't care," she said. "Look, I'm sorry that he's uncomfortable with it, and that's ALL I can say."

And when asked further about Travolta sending his demand letter to Gawker to pull down the post, she said it best!

When she made the statement that by doing so Travolta was just bringing attention to it, and he should have just left it alone, she was dead on. Unfortunately for John, the damage was done, but it was just the beginning of many blessings coming my way in the pursuit of proving the truth to what I had written about JT's secret sex life.

I applaud Ms. Fisher and I thank her for her honesty, after

all she didn't go out and try to "out" Travolta, she simply answered a question honestly when being interviewed.

Her truth and honesty goes to show what length Travolta will go to to lie to his fans and the world as to who he really is. It exposes the fraud in the man.

I have always loved Ms. Fisher's mother, Debbie Reynolds. I have seen every movie she ever made. In particular, I have watched "The Unsinkable Molly Brown" at least twenty times over the years.

It comes as no surprise to me that that movie would resonate with me so strongly.

Molly Brown was a survivor, and when this movie came into my life, I was a young boy looking for someone or something to learn from on how to survive my horrid childhood, and "The Unsinkable Molly Brown" was it.

So it is no wonder that her offspring Carrie would be my hero, it is a surprise! But when I look at it all, it makes sense.

Growing up with such a strong mother certainly rubbed off on her and I adore her for being such a strong example of the truth for so many people.

Carrie Fisher got the truth ball rolling in Hollywood and within time, many celebrities were adding their two cents in on Travolta's lies about his sexuality, Margret Cho and

Rashida Jones, to name a few.

The truth is so easy and not hard at all to remember, John Travolta should be thrilled and honored that all his fellow actor peers kept his lies and sex secrets for decades, while he was able to deceive the world and become a star.

All of Hollywood knew to keep quiet about JT's homosexuality, you can't blame Carrie Fisher for speaking the truth in an interview forty years after knowing the fact.

Especially when Mr. Travolta can't stop going to public spas and having sex and shoving it down everybody's throat to see, and keeping himself in the media with his sex problems and cover ups, makes it so hard for his fellow actors to know what to say.

From: robbyrandolph <robbyrandolph@aol.com>
To: Sarah, My attorney
Subject: Re: Witness list for trial
Date: Mon, Aug 20, 2012 9:31 PM

Sarah,

Here are the others I mentioned. 1 hope you reserve the right for us to add more witnesses later should more become agreeable on my end to work with us?? Is that even possible?

xxxxxxxxxx ex employee Spyglass Hill Golf Course, 1700, 17 mile Dr, Pebble Beach CA, 93953. He worked there for over four years. He contacted me in 2010, telling me he had witnessed Travolta hooking up with guys at the spa on numerous occasions, and that the manager had to repeatedly tell Travolta to stop bothering the guests, who were complaining.

Albert xxxxx, employee on the AT&T Golf Circuit 2010, contacted me, telling me he was happy to see someone standing up to Travolta, because he, along with other guests of the Hotel they were staying in had witnessed the movie star in the steam room, acting perverted and masturbating.

Jay xxxxxxx contacted me in 2010, telling me that he was a boyfriend of Travolta's for a short while after Jett's death in

2009. He says that Travolta and he hooked up at the Olympics in Whistler, BC, and that he was proud of me for coming forward and telling my story and that if I ever needed support relating to Travolta, to contact him. He said he is in fear of Travolta.

Ryan xxxxxxx contacted me in 2010 to let me know that he goes way back with Travolta's sex antics, and that if I ever needed help regarding Travolta & his secrets to let him know.

He says he was very close friends with producer Allan Carr who produced "Grease" and that Allan told him years ago that he made Travolta suck his dick for the lead part that was originally intended for Jeff Conaway. He says Travolta did it and got the lead.

Israel xxxxxxxx contacted me this year 2012 and has sent me over 90 emails relating to Travolta and his legal problems. He has made it clear in the emails that he, too, is in the middle of his own legal problems with Travolta, and I think we should throw his name into the witness list because it will "Ring A Bell" with Travolta, and since he sent almost a hundred emails to me regarding Travolta telling me to stay strong etc, and going into his own issues with him, I think he's good.

Sarah,

This is it for now, Please send me a copy when you're done.

I can't wait. Don't forget! I'm working on a possible five more witnesses and I'm also working on getting last names and addresses for those that are missing them.

Monday is great---can we do it around 12-1-2-3---what works for you? It would be great if I could leave your office in time to beat the traffic back to LA, but other than that I'm totally available to see you Monday, just say when.

Sincerely,

Robert

P.S. When you finish, please send me a copy of what they are getting. I'm super excited now!!!

Wow, I am very impressed with this list!!!

Thank you so much for pulling it together today. I will get to work on this so that we can get it out tonight. I will forward you a copy.

This list, plus the letter from PJ Brant, will get rid of the damages issue. Now the last remaining item is the privilege issue. Having one less item to focus on certainly helps!

Sarah

From: robbyrandolph@aol.com

[mailto:robbyrandolph@aol.com] Sent: Monday, August 20, 2012 6:39 PM

To: Sarah, my attorney

Subject: Re: Witness list for trial against Travolta

Sarah,

Here is my witness list.

Ira Reiner, ex-DA of LA. He was instrumental in keeping City Spa opened during the early eighties when all the "Bath Houses" in LA were being closed over the AIDS scare. He witnessed Travolta's lewd behavior for over three decades at City Spa. I've known him personally from the spa for about 25 years. Over the years, Ira was there plenty of times to witness Travolta sexually on the prowl for fresh victims. Whenever Travolta would come into the spa, Ira would say, 'oh God, not him again', and then he would walk away in disgust. (witness for predator activity)

Carrie Fisher, actress. She came out in my defense against Travolta, when she was asked in an interview about Marty Singer's five page letter about me. She said Travolta had just brought more attention to the matter and that she did not know what the big deal was over John being gay. She said I know he is gay and I'm sorry if he has a problem with it, but it is no secret.

Vicky Lizzy, Jeff Conway's girlfriend at the time of his death, she states that Travolta gave Jeff a BJ while he was sleeping, only to wake up with it happening. She states the incident was so hard for Jeff to get over, and that it bothered him till his death.

Rashida Jones, actress. About a week ago, made a public plea to Travolta to just come out already. She then apologized for making a comment about anybody's private life. She did not retract her statement.

Paul Baressi, Travolta's first boyfriend to come out against him. By the way, he works for Marty Singer doing private investigation work? How weird is that, right?

Author Bruce Headrick, "Tell Secrets Tell No Lies" He has been extremely supportive of me. Since the very first news of my book came out, he has stated on more than one occasion that he is here for me in every way to bring the truth out. He was best friends with Paul Baressi, Travolta's boyfriend at the time, and he says he will tell whoever he needs to the truth.

Musician xxxxxxxxxx He is the guy who wanted to buy the rights to the title of my book for a musical comedy (at the moment he is on the fence), but I will get him to come around.

Charles xxxxxxxxx My friend who witnessed Travolta in lewd behavior at City Spa. On one of my visits to the spa,

Chuck was pursued by Travolta for sex. John opened his towel to Chuck and exposed his penis and masturbated. Chuck walked out in disgust (witnessed predator activity).

Ilya, actor. He is also a friend. I wrote about him in my book. On his first visit to the spa with me, he witnessed Travolta in the shower masturbating.

Detective John Shafia, Wilshire Police Division, 213/xxx-xxxx. He is the Detective who handled the Attack against my life at City Spa. He said when he saw the pictures of the crime scene, it was so bad with all the blood etc, that he put me/my case at the top of his list.

Jeff Katherin, the ex-boyfriend/nanny of Travolta, who found Jett Travolta dead on January 3rd 2009. He is also the guy who was seen in the famous now "Kiss Picture from 2006" and the person I witnessed at the spa with Travolta with his son Jett in January 2007.

Joan Edwards, Travolta's personal secretary from 1978 to 1994, says she witnessed Travolta's six year relationship with Doug Gotterba (I spoke to my source at the magazine. They said she will be an excellent witness, he said she loves to talk and tell the truth).

Doug Gotterba, Travolta's ex-boyfriend, who had a 6 year relationship with Travolta (passed a polygraph about his story).

Luis Gonzalez, former massage therapist at Ritz Carlton

Hotel, Laguna Niguel, CA, had sex with Travolta and told his story to the National Enquirer, because he wanted to expose the truth (he also passed a polygraph about his claim).

Michael Caputo, former Peninsula Hotel employee, shared his story about Travolta's sexually lewd ways with the National Enquirer. He also tells how Travolta was banned from the spa (he also passed a polygraph about his story).

Dr.xxxxxxxxx, D.P.M. He was a member of City Spa for decades. Travolta was after him for years for sex. He cannot stand Travolta and his sex ways. This is the client of Milena Popovitch's that I wrote about in my book (of course I used a different name for him). He is a doctor here in town (he witnessed years of Travolta's predatory activity).

Milena Popovitch, ex-massage therapist from City Spa who is in my book. She witnessed years of his sexual behavior. She is also the person who came up with the WHOLE BOYFRIEND IDEA between Travolta and myself.

Manuel, Chef at City Spa who witnessed years of Travolta's sex antics at the spa. He is also the employee that came up to me back in 2003 after the attack on my life, and he told me how he himself had practically been attacked by Warren Smith around the same time I was, and that Kambiz, the owner, had prior knowledge of Warren's

Coke-fueled rages at the spa and that if I needed him to ever testify to that, he would. I ran into him a couple of weeks ago and he is not working at City Spa any more, so he should be able to talk without fear of losing his job.

Hassan, ex-City Spa massage therapist. He witnessed Travolta cruising for sex at the spa for over ten years. He no longer works there either, so he should talk without too much fear (witnessed Predatory activity).

Nate, current employee at City Spa. I do not have his last name. He is the person I dedicated my book to. I believe he would talk under a subpoena. He is also the person who ran out the front doors in 2003 and saved my life from Warren Smith"s attack against me with a deadly weapon. He told me that he has so much crap on Travolta and his sex at City Spa. I believe this witness will be very unnerving to Travolta, because he has seen so much of John's sex secrets at the spa.

Serge, current employee at City Spa, massage body scrub guy, he is also in my book. He hates Travolta and if under oath, I know he would tell the truth. He calls Travolta a PERVERT who is sick in the head. He has witnessed Travolta cruising for sex at City Spa for years and has a lot to tell.

Vladimir, current employee at City spa and Travolta's massage therapist for over twenty years there. He is also in my book. He was a friend to me for years and he shared a lot with me about Travolta, some of it is in the book, most of it is not.

Joseph, ex-massage therapist at City Spa. He was also Travolta's exclusive massage therapist for years. He witnessed Travolta's lewd behavior at the spa. For years, he also would share with me that all the employees were always having fun at Travolta's expense with his secret sex life.

Solomon Oh, current employee at Century Spa, 4120 W. Olympic Blvd, Los Angeles, CA 90019. He is a massage therapist at Century Spa, who has witnessed Travolta cruising for sex at the spa for over five years.

Mark Riccardi, stuntman, he has witnessed Travolta ruin lives (his own words) on set for over ten years. He sent me an email thanking me for having the balls to face Travolta. He worked with JT for over ten years. He also states he worked privately with Travolta for eight years and that when he would travel with Travolta on trips, he would have to push a cabinet in front of his door to keep Travolta from pushing his way into his Hotel room and molesting him. I met with him for coffee and talk, I found him to be very sincere. He also says he has witnessed Travolta ruin four guys' lives. In particular, one of the guys had a nervous breakdown.

Jennifer. She contacted me in 2010 and shared a story with me regarding TWO of her friends who had husbands that worked in Hollywood. Both of the husbands cheated on their wives with Travolta, and one of the woman actually killed herself over the sex affair her husband had with Travolta (VERY HEAVY).

Daniel, contacted me in 2011 to share with me his story of Travolta. He says that he witnessed Travolta at a party getting his penis sucked by five different guys at the same time at Studio 54 before it closed down, he says they were all "High" and the sex was flowing.

Jonathine. He wrote to me in June of 2011, telling me about his sex hook up with Travolta while John was in town filming a movie, and that he had sex all night with Travolta.

Fernando, ex-Travolta employee, rather her cousin is the ex-employee that worked for both John and Kelly for many years (her words). She says that both Kelly and John had a sexual relationship with her cousin for over a year and that he felt he had no choice but to service both of them sexually if he wanted to keep his job.

Chris, 16 year employee at Ritz Carlton Orlando & Disneyland Hotel concierge for 10 years. Chris wrote to me back in 2010 when the story first broke about my upcoming book. He says he personally worked VIP services for John Travolta for sixteen years and that he witnessed it all. He also says that when Travolta was at the Hotel, the management would put ads on Craigslist to drum up men to come to the spa because John Travolta was there and that after the spa would feel up with guys, Travolta would pick out who he wanted and then the management would make it happen for Travolta. He also says that while giving Travolta massages, John aggressively put the moves on him. He has so many stories to tell, not only about John, but about Kelly as well. He says Kelly would always sit and talk to him after he had massaged John and Kelly would always ask, 'was Johnny a good boy during his massage? or did you need to give him a spanking?' I feel Chris will be a great witness. He says Travolta destroyed his life.

Fabian Zanzi, I think you know his info...

Xxxxxx, actor. He witnessed Travolta engaging in (predatory activity) for many years ... maybe twenty five years now. He is in my book as well. When he would see John, he would always walk away from him, so he wouldn't have to witness Travolta's sex activity.

XXXX, actor. He has witnessed Travolta for years at City Spa and every time he would see Travolta coming, he would make a negative comment about John looking for sex and he would walk away mad. He is in the book

XXX, actor. He has witnessed Travolta and his sex quest at City Spa for many, many years.

I only listed these three actors from the book, because I actually think under oath they might tell the truth about Travolta.

SUING JOHN TRAVOLTA AND MARTY SINGER

I am a survivor of incest molestation that took place throughout my entire childhood until the age of thirteen, I was bullied practically every day I went to school, until I learned to ditch school and hide under the freeway underpass (for safety) till school was out.

 I have paid dearly in my life for the lack of a proper education that my bullies didn't afford me... But I survived!!

When Travolta and his attorney Marty Singer could come up with nothing against me, except lies to defend Travolta's sex addicted life that I had written about, they fucked with the wrong man!

To have survived the things I have shared with you and so much more it took strength, this would come from learning to fight when I was being beaten and realizing that all we really have in this life is who we are.

When it was brought to my attention that Travolta had put out a five page letter of lies about me for the world to read, I was ready to fight. The greatest thing about a fight is when you have the truth on your side and so much of the truth can really kick your attacker's ass!

The only thing Marty Singer could do was attack me personally with his made-up lies... He never once made a single statement refuting what was in the book about his client? The fact that Travolta never sued me says it all and the world can see that.

As long as I can draw my own breath, I will never let anyone, famous or not, state lies about me in any form.

After all, my integrity and reputation means everything to me.

So I knew I would address his five pages of lies when I felt better. In the meantime, I was deep in shock, having just learned weeks earlier of my father's suicide.

I do believe everything in life happens for a reason, with many different outcomes that can come from a single situation.

I guess what I am trying to say here is, though Travolta set out with lies to destroy me with his stupid letter, he didn't, and in many ways he put me on the map!

I released two hundred and twenty pages of truth about John Travolta and his sex life in public spas in my book YNSITTA and he did not sue me for one word of what I wrote.

He puts out five pages of bullshit on me, and you better believe I am going to be suing not only Travolta, but his legal puppet, Marty Singer, as well.

The fact that the judge would not allow my lawsuit to go forward was no shock to me.

I knew the chances were very slim due to the "Privilege" bullshit Marty likes to hide behind with his assaults through "Privileged" letters that he leaks to the media---all designed to attack and destroy.

The facts stand on their own and so does both of my books, "You'll Never spa In This Town Again" and now "Tracking Travolta" and shortly so will "Tracking Travolta 2".

Nobody from the spas I wrote about, famous or not, came to Travolta's defense when my book came out, because nobody was going to be speaking up for him when they all had witnessed his deviant sexual behavior for years as well. Not one person went on the record in Travolta's defense or behalf.

I decided to include for you to see the actual witness list I had prepared against Travolta for our day in court, had it ever come. This is the one forwarded to Singer and Travolta to go over.

There were thirty nine witnesses we were prepared to call to testify against Travolta.

In time, I would have well over one hundred and fifty potential witnesses to testify to the truth of JT's sexuality and what I was claiming.

When the time came for both law suits to be served on Travolta---mine and Fabian's, it was fun to see him on the run... The big movie star was acting just like the rest of us do when we are going to be served with a lawsuit against us, scared.

He was hiding inside his house and he knew the process servers were waiting for him outside. I couldn't help but feel a true sense of pride that this day had come.

To get Fabian to justice with an attorney to sue Travolta was absolutely the hardest thing to pull off, but I did, and it was down to the last few days before his lawsuit would have been no good, due to the statue of limitations running out, and to have my lawsuit here being served on Travolta for his lies about me, it was a great day indeed!

Subject: TMZ
From: Morgan <Morganxxxxx@tmz.com>
Date: Wed, May 09, 2012 10:18 am
To: "info@youllneverspainthistownagain.com"

Hi Robert,

My name's Morgan and I work at TMZ here in Los Angeles. I came across your website and would love to talk with you about your books. If you could please give me a call as soon as possible, I'd really appreciate it! My number is xxxxxxxxx. Thanks so much!

Sincerely,

Morgan

Sent: Friday, May 11, 2012 5:36 PM
To: Morgan at TMZ
Subject: RE: As Promised!!

Morgan,

I hope you are enjoying your SICK day LOL. I promised I would send you some information to use, so here goes.

My book sales have gone up 1000% and rising every day since the Scandal broke.

Also, I'm now FREE to talk about victim number #3 Fabian Zanzi who has come forward. I have known him for the last year and a half and I have been actively been trying to help him, since he seeked me out for help. I also include a brief description of what Fabian went through at the end of my book "You'll Never Spa In This Town Again". I also have four other victims that I have been in contact with, that I am trying to convince to come forward.

On Monday I will be doing CBS INSIDER, and a ton of other shows. But I would love to give you and TMZ some information that nobody has yet. I would love to do TMZ live?? So let me know your thoughts ASAP, because I'm being hounded by reporters and I don't want to leave them hanging...

I told you I would give you first shot ... Here it is!!

Sincerely

Author Robert Randolph

TRACKING TRAVOLTA

Subject: Re: As Promised!!
From: Morgan Morganxxxxxxx@tmz.com
Date: Tue, May 15, 2012 8:44 PM
To: info@youlineverspainthistownagain.com

Hey Robert---please send over the numbers when you get a chance tonight! I just need how many books you were selling before the Travolta story broke and also after it broke. And also would like to know what the price of a book is. I'm going to need to show my boss first thing in the morning when I get in at 6AM! Thank you so so so much.

TRACKING TRAVOLTA

Subject:
From: info@youllneverspainthistownagain.com
Date: Tue, May 15, 2012 10:14 PM
To: Morgan <Morganxxxxxxx@tmz.com>

Morgan,

Hi, I'm sorry it took me so long to get back to you. You know I have given it some more thought and as I told you my sales have gone up 1000% and they're still climbing with every day, but I have decided I'm not comfortable saying my exact book number, for many reasons. It's nothing personal!!! The book is $15.25

Thanks for trying to get me some extra PR for my book!! Maybe next time... huh… It was a pleasure talking with you regarding everything...

Take care

Robert

Subject: RE: As Promised!!
From: Morgan Morganxxxxxxx@tmz.com
Date: Tue, May 15, 2012 10:23 am
To: "info@youllneverspainthistownagain.com" <info@youllneverspainthistownagain.com>

Thanks for your email, Robert! Sorry I couldn't get back to you sooner.

What exactly does 1000% mean? Do you have numbers for sales pre and post scandal? Is there are chart or a graph or anything. My bosses think this is a great story and want to run it as long as we have some more of an idea about the numbers of sales.

And we won't include anything else about your connection to victims until you are allowed to talk again.

Please let me know ASAP!!!

Thanks again! And if you have any questions, feel free to give me a call!

Morgan

Subject: RE: TMZ
From: info@youllneverspainthistownagain.com
Date: Sun, May13, 2012 6:41 PM

To: Morgan

Morgan,

Hi, I hope you are enjoying the day!!

I wanted to give you an update. I have been advised by my Attorney's that until Fabian Zanzi and these other victims (that I am personally aware of) file their lawsuits, it would be in everybody's best interest if I don't do any further talking.

I have cancelled all my interviews for this upcoming week, and until I'm told differently, I have to keep quiet. Please feel free to use anything I have shared with you up till now. If you want to…

Take care.

Robert Randolph

TMZ

I love TMZ, even if they tricked me into giving up Fabian Zanzi's location so they could get an interview from him.

I had spoken to Morgan, one of the reporters at TMZ several times, regarding my book YNSITTA and she was always cool with me.

When Travolta's sex scandal was at its height, every reporter on the planet wanted to speak to the "Cruise ship worker" who had come forward in Chile and told his story of sexual assault to the people of Chile.

Nobody could find him and Travolta was in hiding. This is where Morgan comes in, she reaches out to me to talk about what was going on with Travolta and everybody that was coming forward to accuse him of sexual assault and I told her where Fabian was hiding.

TMZ took the information I gave them and sent one of their correspondences to interview Fabian.

I don't mind that they got to him first because of what I told them, just wish it could have been better for Fabian. He had no money at all, and since Travolta had done this to his life with his sex attack against him, he deserved something.

I secured for Fabian a deal with a magazine for $50,000.00 US dollars and all he had to do was talk on the phone through me with the magazine and the money was going to be his (he so desperately needed it too!) but instead, TMZ took the info I so honestly gave them and located Fabian, and the rest is history.

When I spoke to Fabian after I saw the interview, he was worried I might be upset with him for talking, I was but only because I knew he didn't know better about the $ amount his interview was worth.

When I asked how much TMZ gave him, he said $1,000.00. They are in the business of telling stories and buying stories as well if they choose to, and the point that they get it for the least amount of money possible is just business for them and it is normal. It was personal for me.

I had Fabian's best interest at heart and one thousand bucks was not going to do much to help his life.

I didn't know what I was going to do now to help this poor kid who Travolta destroyed with his actions. He had now given away his story for peanuts, so there was no hope of rebuilding his life from interview money, etc. I really was disappointed that TMZ beat me to the punch with my own information to them.

I would not rest till I figured out another possible solution for Fabian, it would take time before it would come to me.

Like I said before, I like TMZ , and I think Harvey Levine is a great man to look up to for LGBTs and everybody in between. I know that for a fact---that he shares the truth of his life with his viewers to make a difference.

Gay men of power like Harvey Levine are changing the world with their honesty of life that they share with us all. When I was growing up, I did not have a Harvey Levine to look up to or a Ellen DeGeneres there to be known.

I know these kids today are going to have better lives because of the Harvey Levines and Ellens of the world!

Subject: Info on John Travolta's boyfriend
From: xxxxxxxxxxxxxxx
Date: March 21, 2012
To: info@youllneverspainthistownagain.com

Hello,

I have been watching your story progress in the National Enquirer regarding your upcoming book. I would like to share a story with you about a pilot who was involved with John Travolta for many years. I don't prefer emails. If you are interested in more details, please call only. Xxxxxxxxxxxxxxxx up till midnight most nights.
Thanks.

DOUG GOTTERBA

"When he doesn't like you anymore, he will wish you into the corn field".

That is the line in the famous "Twilight Zone" episode where Billy Mummy wishes everyone he doesn't like into the corn field. That is what comes to mind when I think of what came of Doug Gotterba, John's pilot boyfriend that has disappeared.

"Travoltanized" is what I call it.

I feel bad for Doug that he won't be able to continue to tell his story about his relationship with Travolta. I followed Doug on Twitter and he was really geared up to go forward with his story as long as he won his case against Travolta in court, but unfortunately for Doug, he lost, and has been silenced.

I was looking forward to having him tell his story and having another person on the truth circuit with me regarding Travolta, but that is not to be.

Doug almost had him, but unfortunately the confidentiality agreement that he signed when he got his job with Travolta will stand in place, and honestly, I have to say that I thought that was the way it was going to go for him, although I had hoped for a different outcome.

When I learned the facts of the confidentiality agreement, it was pretty clear to me that Travolta's attorney would shut Gotterba down.

After all, the affair took place while he was under employment to Travolta and though it's clear with all the pictures of the two together that they were lovers, he was still under contract to keep quiet, and we all know keep quiet he did not.

Though Gotterba will not be going on to tell the rest of his story, he at least left his mark on Travolta's biography, that has to bring him some satisfaction I would think.

It promised to be a really good read and who knows it may have gone on to see the kind of success that Liberace's book by his former lover had. Unfortunately, we will never know, because Mr. Gotterba has been Travoltanized into the corn field of silence, a place many of Travolta's enemies go to, like his body double Mark Riccardi and so forth...

I first learned of Doug Gotterba from a man who was claiming to be Doug's old boyfriend. He sent me a brief email wanting to talk about how I thought he should go about getting his boyfriend some help spreading the word about Travolta.

He made claims that Doug had a video tape of he and JT in a hotel room and that his boyfriend was a pilot and had been involved with Travolta for six years.

I called the number he gave me in the email and we spoke, he claimed to be Doug's current boyfriend and was trying to persuade Doug to come forward to the media with the affair.

I asked him what was on the tape?, he said Doug only showed him a part where Travolta was standing in a hotel room in his underwear.

"That's all he would show me of the tape."

"It was definitely Travolta."

He said that he waited one day till Doug was gone on a flight and he went into the safe and watched the tape, "It was a very soft kind of tape" he said, when you watch them together you can tell they are in love so its kinda sappy that way... No real heavy stuff, just Doug and Travolta making out.

The guy said John was definitely a very effeminate man in the tape and that he was rather shocked to see that, he also said he was shocked to learn with his own eyes that Travolta was indeed gay.. He told me that he really felt Doug wanted him to watch the tape.

"Why else would he tell me where it was before he went out of town?" This guy also made it clear that Doug was not looking to go public with this information.

I told him that I thought he should start with the National Enquirer and gave him my connections there to talk to. He claimed that Doug was a really nice man and he had truly fallen in love with Travolta and still carried a torch for him. He also stated the only reason Doug would even consider coming forward would be because he was so sick of Travolta lying to the world about his homosexuality and every time he heard John deny he was gay it made him sick.

He made it very clear to me that Doug could not come forward on his own because he had signed a privacy agreement with Travolta. He said that's when he and Doug came up with the idea for leaking the story as if Doug had nothing to do with it, "But he did!" he was not an unwilling participant in this news coming out, so the boyfriend said.

Within a month from talking with this guy, I was seeing Doug's picture and story everywhere. I was really excited to see someone come forward about Travolta and finally put their name and face behind what they were saying, up till this time I was still the only one who had done so.

I kept thinking how great this was going to be with Doug's story crossing the globe and making worldwide news.

Unfortunately, it wasn't too much later that I started to hear that Marty Singer was going to be shutting this boyfriend down from telling the world his whole story, in his upcoming book he was working on.

Again the problem here is that Doug had signed that confidentiality agreement that would ultimately make it impossible to go forward with his book.

I kept tabs on Doug through his Twitter account and boy, was he ready to give it to Travolta. He was busy having his book written for him, and was constantly tweeting his progress and updates. As his court day grew closer with Travolta, you could read the excitement in Doug's tweets to finally have his day in court with the "*Face Off*" star.

Up till then, Doug was telling us how he was going to expose the truth of the six year love affair the two men shared. I came away with the feeling that Doug Gotterba is a real nice man from what I learned about him. I received many emails regarding Doug and Travolta's affair from those claiming to have been there while it blossomed.

His day in court came and he lost. Shortly thereafter, Doug was "Travoltanized" and day by day, Doug's social media world got smaller and smaller, and Travolta's presence in Doug's life was removed.

When I checked out Doug's Twitter page after the court ruling, all mention of his upcoming book and his affair with Travolta was gone.

He hasn't tweeted anymore and it appears that Mr. Gotterba has been "Travoltanized" for good by his old flame.

I wish Doug the best and I hope in some way my writing about him and including his story in my book gives him some sort of satisfaction.

I am still on the bench as to whether I will write further about Travolta and Gotterba's affair. I mean just because Gotterba has been silenced doesn't mean I have, and as I said earlier, I was contacted by an interesting little group of people that were very close to both the movie star and the pilot as their love grew.

JT and Gotterba took several exotic trips together during their affair. For now it is a story that has come to an end unless someone resurrects it later on, and in Hollywood, those things happen all the time.

UPDATE: I am beyond thrilled to see Mr. Gotterba has won his appeal against Travolta…WOW! Way to go Doug! I am pulling for you!...Though I was told you have already reached a settlement with Travolta to go no further.

TRACKING TRAVOLTA

From: Sarah J. Golden, Esq.XXXXXXXXXXXX
To: robbyrandolph <robbyrandolph@aol.com>
Cc: 'Servando Timbol' XXXXXXXXXXX
Subject: RE: checking in
Date: Wed, Jun 13, 2012 11:48 AM

Hi Robert;

Good morning! I want to file the lawsuits either this Friday or Monday the 18th at the latest. I am supposed to speak with Fabian's psychiatrist today to request the appropriate records.

That is the last piece of information holding up the suit. If the doctor is able to articulate to me the contents in the records, then I do not need to wait for the documentation. The point is just to make sure that Fabian told the doctor about the incident in July of 2009.

If the doc can verify that over the phone, then I can make the allegation in the lawsuit under the emotional distress causes of action.

If you speak with Vince and Ryan, let them know that after we file the lawsuit, there will be a lot of mud-slinging in the media. Travolta's team will be making discrediting statements in the media about you, Fabian, and the law firm.

I do not want them to think poorly of the lawsuits, just because Marty says they are crap.

Marty may also get other attorneys/witnesses to comment on the veracity of our claims. These slimeballs will stop at nothing. I do not want these media comments to sway their decision to come forward - either with our firm or another firm.

I will send you an email regarding your lawsuit. Then if you have any questions, we can have a conference call if that is more convenient than meeting in person (although it is always nice to see you!).

I will be working on that email today and/or tomorrow.

With respect to Chris, the statute of limitations will likely bar his case, unless there is some sort of latent delayed emotional distress that occurred recently. The only way to delay the statute of limitations is if a person did not have the ability to discover the injury.

For instance, if someone drafts a will incorrectly, the discovery of the error will not occur until the drafter dies. With your case, we can delay the statute of limitations, because you were not financially damaged until you released the book in 2012.

It is hard to delay a sexual battery/assault claim because the victim is damaged right away and knows it. The statute will not delay even if someone is scared of losing his job. It is really unfair, but that is the way the law sees it.

Next time we speak, let me know the details of Chris' case and we can see if there is anything that can be done. In the meantime, keep Chris handy as a witness for Travolta's sexual crimes. If he is willing to testify regarding Travolta's propensities, then perhaps he can help past victims and future victims as well.

Sarah

From: robbyrandolph <robbyrandolph@aol.com>
To: Sarah my attorney
Subject: Re: checking in
Date: Tue, Jun 12, 2012 4:26 PM

Sarah,

Thanks for the update. When I met with Ryan and Vince, they both said they would sit tight till we filed the suits. I expect that after we file my and Fabian's suit, that they will come forward to file theirs. I feel very strongly that if they do go forward, they will come to your firm.

They both made it clear to me that they had not spoken to any other Attorney about their possible cases. So I think we will have them on board soon. Do you have a rough idea as to when you might be filing the suits?

I think when we did not file as we said, it made them a little more cautious for the moment, but once we do (file), I feel strongly about BOTH of them. It sounds like the suit for Fabian is going to be much STRONGER now!!

If you need anything, please let me know.

Sincerely

Robert

P.S. I am talking with this Chris guy that I told you about, the one who was assaulted by Travolta many times while he worked at the Disneyland concierge.

The question I have for you is.... Can a person still sue for damages after their statute has passed?? If the reason they did not do anything was out of fear of Travolta retaliating against them at the time??

He wants to possibly sue Travolta for what he put him through... but his concern is that it has been almost 4 years since his last encounter with JT??

So I was wondering can he still sue for some other thing??? He says that he put up with JT's sexual advances for several years... I think he said for six years he kept his mouth shut for fear of losing his job??

Please give it some thought. I told him I would get back to him by Friday.

-----Original Message-----
From: Sarah J. Golden, Esq. XXXXXXXXXXX
To: robbyrandolph <robbyrandolph@aol.com>
Sent: Tue, Jun 12, 2012 1:49 PM
Subject: RE: checking in

Hi Robert;

Thanks for checking in. We're still working on the additions for Fabian's lawsuit. I am getting very excited, as I think the additions really do a great job explaining the whole story. I am just picturing Marty Singer's face when he sees that we have addressed all the negative and he has nothing to leak!

Are we still on for tomorrow afternoon for you, Vince, and Ryan? We can meet with you earlier to go over a few things with your lawsuit - nothing major. Let me know if you have any questions. Happy moving!

Sarah

Sarah J. Golden, Esq

Golden & Timbol, A Professional Law Corporation

xxxxxxxxxxxxxxxxxxxxxxxxxxx

xxxxxxxxxxxxxxxxxxxxxxxxxxx

"TRACKING TRAVOLTA 3"

Vince and Ryan's story

Just when you thought you heard it ALL!

COMING SOON

As you see by the proceeding emails between my attorney and I regarding Travolta, I was seeking advice and help for Fabian Zanzi, Chris Williams, and Vince and Ryan. Keep in mind this is only a fraction of the men that I tried to get help for in one way or another, who fell prey to Travolta's unwanted sexual advances, ultimately leading up to some horrific ending of sorts for all these men.

The only common thread here was they were all men, and most of them were unhappy with JT, not just for going a little too far, but because he assaulted sexually these men and touched many of them with his erect penis as you can read about in countless lawsuits pertaining to the very thing I am saying.

They all said John Travolta does not like to hear the word no.

Of the men mentioned in the email Fabian and Chris went on to sue Travolta, in Chris's case, he named Travolta in his suit but sued the "Ritz Carlton" in Orlando for what JT put him through. He ultimately ended up settling for pennies on the dollar as he said.

Then there is Vince and Ryan they were both looking to sue Travolta for his sexual misconduct and the attack. They both say they barely survived while away with the "Swordfish" star on an all men only get away that went terribly wrong. When I heard all the details of their story, I was floored and remember it takes a lot to floor me!

We decided the way Travolta was making a joke of so many of the men he had assaulted and the way his Attorney, Marty Singer, was attacking these innocent victims for coming forward was horrific, so they decided to tell me their story in full and let the world know what they went through with the movie star through me and spare themselves the "Side Show" Travolta's people make of everyone.

Travolta most definitely would be behind bars for what they told me he did to them.

It is one thing when both, or all, the adults are consenting sexual partners to the fun and games, but apparently on the weekend of the attacks in question, Travolta took things to a whole new level.

The latest craze in Hollywood and around the world these days is S&M, with such hit books as *50 Shades of Grey* being made into a movie.

Travolta's '50 Shades of Gay' would be more like it from what I listened to from both these good-looking men.

If things had gone as Vince and Ryan were planning for that getaway there would be no story, but it didn't go like they were promised and were paid for. And paid well they were from what they said, but even so, would that give Travolta the right to take things to the extreme he did?

The answer is no. There is no dollar amount that would make what he put them through worth it.

I asked them both why when they finally broke free and got away from Travolta's clutches within minutes of losing their lives, didn't they go right to the cops?

What they told me made the hair on the back of my neck stand up.

I knew they were indeed telling me the truth they had all their facts straight and they had taken pictures of their bruised torsos that John so mercilessly beat during the "Sex Games".

Auto asphyxiation is apparently something the "Saturday Night Fever" star knows a lot about, like his fellow 70's TV icon David Carradine from Kung Fu fame. We all know how it ended up for Carradine.

I wonder why Travolta would even go near this crazy new sex game of auto asphyxiation.

Vince and Ryan were both paid pros in this getaway of Travolta's, but that doesn't take away from the fact that they had the right to say NO and when they did, he didn't.

Read what these men had to do to get away and find out how they succeeded in overcoming the trauma that Travolta scared them with, in Tracking Travolta 3.

Subject: Travolta tell all
From: xxxxxxxxxxx
Date: xxxxxxxxxxxxxxxx
To: info@youllneverspainthistownagain.com

Mr. Randolph,

I have known, for years, that John Travolta is a hypocrite homosexual living a lie!!!

I fooled around with him on three occasions. Always at the spa in your book, City Spa. My last time with him was in 2008. All three times, it was pretty much the same. Mutual blowjobs to each other. But the last time in 2008, Mr. Travolta showed a lot of interest in my ass. I told him I'm not into anal action. He said that was cool… but he was. I left it at that. I haven't seen him since then.

I bet with your book coming, everyone will be seeing less of him at the spas. I personally will miss that! It was always so much fun to see the world's biggest movie star getting down and dirty like the rest of us. When do you anticipate your release date?

Take care.

Subject: book

From: xxxxxxxxxxx

Date: xxxxxxxxxxx

To: info@youllneverspainthistownagain.com

To whom it may concern:

Who does John Travolta think he is fooling????

He's as gay as you get. My friends and I have seen him over the last ten years at spas in L.A. and he is always doing the same thing, playing with his dick and looking for men. Two of my friends had sex with him right inside the spa. He never wanted me, as I am overweight.

But when they were done with Travolta, they both said he is "insatiable".

Maybe if I lost some weight, I could get some Travolta sex, too.

Hope you sell a million books.

Subject: Some info and some editing
From: xxxxxxxxxxx
Date: Wednesday, October 20, 2010 2:38PM
To: info@youllneverspainthistownagain.com

Many MANY years ago, Ravolta blamed his former NYC manager for his queer rumors. The guy was dead by then (Bob LeMond) but had a rep for being a little sleazy --- most of his clients were 20's cute boys and he had a partner named Lois Zetter (a female who gave him some hetero-legitimacy) --- so Ravolta's reps told the press that the gay association shit was because he had a gay manager. Real nice: maligning the dead.

In your "bio" page, you mean "aid," not "aide."

There are other typos too, but this one is sort of glaring.

I hope you don't get run off the road permanently. Sounds like you should be in hiding.

Be safe.

Subject: Book Order

From: xxxxxxxxxxx

Date: Friday, November 19, 2012 2:30 PM

To: info@youllneverspainthistownagain.com

Hi there.

Is your book available on line yet or is it just copies of the printed book you're taking orders for? John is a kind of sad character who was in love with a guy on the set of Hairspray when he was up here in Toronto filming a few years ago. He's even offered to pay for the straight guy to come visit him in the U.S... I'd love to read about the celebs you've bumped into. ;)

Keep well.

Subject: looking forward to reading
From: xxxxxxxxxxx
Date: 10/22/2012 12:45 PM
To: robbyrandolph@aol.com

I had heard about John Travolta about 40 years ago. I met Hollywood Producer Allan Carr (in a party) who knew John from Grease. I guess Allan Carr died of AIDS some years back. He had made mention about John, but I didn't believe it until I picked up the Enquirer yesterday and read the story about your forthcoming book. I congratulate you for your bravery in telling it like it is. There is so much hypocrisy out there and maybe this will demonstrate to the public that a lot of these guys are just jerks. I feel sorry for Kelly Preston. She seems like such a decent person. I look towards the forthcoming publication of this book. Rest assured, I will tell my friends about it. Will it be available via amazon.com or should we order from your website? Thanks again for your bravery. I wish you well.

Subject:
From: xxxxxxxxxxx
Date: Saturday, July 28, 2012 4:59 PM
To: info@youllneverspainthistownagain.com

Robert

We have talked long before all these lawsuits and adventures, so I humbly request that we take our friendship to the next level. Before I sign up with your guy, I need a little more info. Are you guys actually getting Singer to settle or is this war just starting?

I know you're under a confidentiality agreement, but I would like to know what I am joining up with. Are you and Fabian settled or is this crap still up in the air?

Just send me a separate email, not attached to anything, with just an 's' for settled or 'u' for up in the air. Then I would know a little to make my next decision and I doubt an 's' or a 'u' in an email by itself is evidence of anything, but I will know.

Subject: Re: My book
From: Chris xxxxxxxxxxxxxxx
Date: Fri, March 09, 2012 10: 16 PM
To: <info@youllneverspainthistownagain.com>

Hi Rob,

I just finished reading your book. The first thing that entered my mind was a line from the movie Camp: "Never meet your heroes because they always disappoint you!" I can see this held true for you and Mr. Travolta.

I have experienced the same situation. I can't say I have been to any of the spas here in the L.A. area, but after my experiences in San Diego spas and Palm Springs resorts, I could relate to a lot of the experiences you expressed in your book.

Meeting stars myself, I have no reason to doubt a single word you have written. I had heard the rumors for years about John from friends and others.

I have worked with other authors in the past through our company. We are currently working with a gay author assisting him in getting his novel turned into a movie, so I know the difference between good writing and storytelling and bad.

In my opinion, I can honestly say I found your book to be well written, easy to follow, and told in a very matter of fact way.

Very few authors, especially first time authors who are writing a non-fiction book, have this talent. I will be sure to recommend it to my friends and associates.

I wish you well in your next publication and will be sure to also purchase it as soon as it becomes available.

All my best,

Chris

From: <info@youllneverspainthistownagain.com>
Date: Sat, 10 Mar 2012 01:23:04 -0700
To: Chris xxxxxxxxxxxxxx
Subject: RE: My book

Chris,

WOW!!!

You truly made my day!!

What a nice person you are to take the time to write to me such wonderful words.

I can only hope that I live up to half of what you wrote...

Your email to me is going down as one of the most touching I have ever received. ..

Thank you!

Subject Hey!
From: Leon xxxxxxxxxxxxx
Date: Wed, Mar 14, 2012 4:11 AM
To: <info@youllneverspainthistownagain.com>

Hey there, I don't know if you answer personal emails any more after reading your incredible ordeal with the death-threaters and other anonymous assholes, it wouldn't shock me, but I was wondering if it's still possible to get your book from your website. I write to you about this because your site says 'pre-order', and I know it should've long been released since 2010, so does that 'pre-order' really mean 'order'? If I can get a copy of your book, that would be great, because I've already searched all over the web and there are nothing but 'reviews' and gay blog site entries, but no place other than your site for attaining a copy.

Just on a personal note, I find your revelations fascinating and I commend you for being so brave through all of this! It must've been a real trial to go ahead and publish a tell-all about those guys... some of them completely shocking (John Cusack! Paul Giamatti!) but ultimately, it doesn't surprise me that so much of Hollywood is so closeted. I heard James Woods is packing a huge dick, and this comes from a gay friend I had years ago...

He saw James in a bathroom taking a piss. Don't know if he is gay though, but like I said, so much of Hollywood is in real denial of their proclivities. I say it's a corporate decision for many of those guys, and by that I mean if they admitted to their homosexuality, their movies wouldn't sell as well, especially in the red states. It's sad.

Well, I really do hope to read your book sometime and I hope the death-threats and all of that shit has stopped for you, because no one should have to live like that! Just goes to show, those guys are only angry because there must be more than a kernel of truth in what you've written!

Sincerely,

Leon

Subject: Hi
From: xxxxxxxxxxxxxx
Date: Tue, Nov 30, 2012 6:06 PM
To: <info@youllneverspainthistownagain.com>

Hi. I'm from Rio de Janeiro and I came to know about John Travolta's manly stuff. I got curious about reading the whole story about him and his hook-ups. I do believe in you. It's no surprise for me to know that a man is in the closet. There are so many ordinary men out there who hide their sexuality and marry a foolish woman to make sure their closets are securely closed. It would be no different about the famous people.

Subject: JOHN REVOLTA
From: Jo xxxxxxxxxxxxxx
Date: Sun, Sep 05, 2012 8:03 PM
To: info@youllneverspainthistownagain.com

Congrats on exposing the hypocrisy. It's creepy that Travolta feels he has to be in the closet and just can't free his soul...1 would figure if someone were gay, to be going on hiding it for decades and fronting a hoax would be a lot of stress .. Why not just be out? Especially now that he's a multi-millionaire! I mean what has he got to lose?

I hope you have photos of the men you claim went to this spa. It's one thing to be attracted to people of the same gender. It's another I to have a promiscuous, sex addicted life. That's sick. It's sicker to be in the closet about it.

From: Sarah J. Golden, Esq.
To: robbyrandolph <robbyrandolph@aol.com>
Subject: RE: Letter from Laveley/Singer and Subsequent Response Date: Fri, Jun 22, 2012 5:46 PM

Robert;

Thank you! These Travolta people are absolutely crazy. I have to wonder if they believe their own lies... absolutely nuts!

Have a great weekend. Call my cell phone if you need anything at all. Talk to you soon!

Sarah

Sarah J. Golden, Esq.
Golden & Timbol, A Professional Law Corporation
xxxxxxxxxxxxxxxxxxxxx
xxxxxxxxxxxxxxxxxxxxxxxxxx

-Original Message--

From: Sarah J. Golden, Esq.
To: robbyrandolph <robbyrandolph@aol.com>
Sent: Fri, Jun 22, 2012 5:32 PM
Subject: Letter from Laveley/Singer and Subsequent Response

Hi Robert;

We received this little gem from Lynda Goldman. Please read my response and provide any feedback. Thank you!

Sarah

Sarah J. Golden, Esq
Golden & Timbol, A Professional Law Corporation
xxxxxxxxxxxxxxxxxxxx
xxxxxxxxxxxxxxxxxxxxxxxx

TRACKING TRAVOLTA

From: robbyrandolph@aol.com

To: Sarah my attorney

Sent: xxxxxxxxxxx

RE: letter from Laveley/Singer and Subsequent Response

I knew I was right when I choose you and your partners to "Take on Travolta". Your letter to Linda is "Classic". You handle yourself so well, and it shines through. I'm super excited at how this is going down. I'm here if you need anything. I hope you have a wonderful weekend and get ready for this upcoming week. It should be real interesting what goes down next week.

I'm so impressed with the way you are handling everything, and I plan on passing that on to Ryan & Vince.

Sincerely

Robert

P.S. l loved your remark to Linda regarding the possibility of another process server at Travolta's house, instead of yours ... LMAO!!!!

It is very clear that you are not going to be pushed around by them... I'm super proud of all of you!!!!!!

LAVELY & SINGER PROFESSIONAL CORPORATION
JOHN H. LAVELY, JR., MARTIN O. SINGER, BRIAN
G. WOLF, LYNDA B. GOLDMAN, MICHAEL D.
HOLTZ, WILLIAM J. BRIGGS, II, PAUL N. SORRELL,
MICHAEL E. WEINSTEN, EVAN N. SPIEGEL

VIA EMAIL:

ATTORNEYS AT LAW
SUITE 2400, 2049 CENTURY PARK EAST, LOS
ANGELES, CALIFORNIA 90067-2906

JUNE 22, 2012

TODD STANFORD EAGAN, HENRY L. SELF, III,
ANDREW B. BRETTLER, DAVID B. JONELIS,
MICHAEL V. MANCINI, ALLISON S. HART, KEVIN
JAMES, OF COUNSEL

Sarah J. Golden, Esq.
Golden & Timbol, P.C.
xxxxxxxxxxxxxxxxx
xxxxxxxxxxxxxxxx

Re: John Travolta adv. Fabian Zanzi. et al.

Our File No.: 1027-171

Dear Ms. Golden:

We are aware of the lawsuit you filed on behalf of Fabian Zanzi against our client. We are authorized to accept service of that Complaint on Mr. Travolta's behalf. However, your process server refused to leave my client's property, notwithstanding the fact that I notified you both in writing and via voicemail last night that we were authorized to accept service on behalf of our client. This is outrageous. We demand that you immediately notify your process server that my office is authorized to accept service on behalf of Mr. Travolta, and immediately instruct your process server not to return to my client's property.

Your process server's refusal to leave my client's property even after you were informed that my office would accept service is harassing and abusive. Any continued unnecessary efforts to serve my client notwithstanding our agreement to accept service on his behalf gives rise to claims for abuse of process. As I informed you last night, we have been authorized to file suit for abuse of process if this outrageous harassment of my client continues.

I trust that you will now promptly call off your process server, and will have the papers delivered to my office so that I may accept service on behalf of my client.

If you disregard this letter, you do so at your peril.

GOLDEN@TIMBOL

A PROFESSIONAL LAW CORPORATION

June 22, 2012

Lynda B. Goldman

LAVELY & SINGER

2049 Century Park East, Suite 2400

Los Angeles, CA 90067

Via U.S.Mail and Email

RE: Randolph v. Travolta, et al.; Zanzi v. Travolta, et al.

Ms. Goldman;

My office is in receipt of your June 22, 2012 letter regarding your office's request to accept service on behalf of Mr. Travolta.

Under California Code of Civil Procedure 415.10, "a summons may be served by personal delivery of a copy of the summons and of the complaint to the person to be served. Service of a summons in this manner is deemed complete at the time of such delivery."

Complying with the California law is hardly "harassing and abusive".

Moreover, if Mr. Travolta did not wish to be served, then he and his staff members should not have advised our process server to wait at the property until Mr. Travolta returned later that evening.

Our process sever was following the instructions that came directly from your client and his agents.

In the future, we kindly request that you communicate with your client and make sure that he is on the same page as you prior to pointing the finger at the wrong party and sending ill informed correspondence to our office.

Finally, your office emailed a letter on June 21, 2012 at 6:59 p.m. requesting that we "call off our process server". My office immediately contacted our process server who promptly left your client's premises at 7:13 p.m.

The mere fourteen minutes that passed from the time your email was received and the time that the processor server left cannot be construed even in the most favorable light as "harassing and abusive".

If a process server was at your client's house after 7:13 p.m., it was not my agent. Perhaps yet another victim is attempting to serve your client as well. Please check your facts.

We sincerely hope that during the pendency of these lawsuits, the catty and unnecessary correspondence filled with incorrect accusations will cease. As a duty to our profession, we are expected to act like professionals. Please keep that in mind during the litigation period.

Please do not hesitate to contact my office if you have any questions.

Sincerely;

Sarah J. Golden, Esq.

XXXXXXXXXXXXXXXXXXXXXXXXXXXXXXXXXXXX

2013

With the "Massage Scandal" finally dying down, my life has been able to get back to a more predictable schedule. I continue to try and get help for victims of Travolta's as they contact me.

I refer them to a wonderful attorney out of Chicago, Michael Bressler, who I have had the pleasure of knowing since he first reached out to me years ago regarding Travolta.

The emails continue to surprise me, you would think when you have heard the similar thing over and over again, that it would desensitize you to it, but it doesn't.

As long as these men seek me out, I will be here to listen and try to help them.

"You know, I would hope that he would be able to be himself.
It's not even like I'm outing him, because it's so obvious.

That's like outing Liberace.

All I'm doing is taking public speculation and joining it with what I know
to be true!"

Comedienne/Actress Margret Cho, 2013

JOEY TRAVOLTA "THE TRUE STAR OF THE FAMILY"

Can you imagine what it must have been like to have grown up in the Travolta house? The Father, a well respected business man, "Tires" and the Mother, an acting coach/teacher.

To me, it seems like it would have been so much fun, there where brothers and sisters everywhere just like you would expect in a true Italian family.

To have their mother teaching them a skill in the art of acting, that would bring most all of the children time in the limelight. WOW! is what comes to mind.

We all know who became the star of the family and who put the family on the Hollywood map, the baby of the bunch John, but what most people in the world don't know is that Joey Travolta is the true star of the family in a way that is so pure and so inspirational to us all.

The more I learned of the older brother to John, that they used to say could never live up to his younger brother John's stardom, the more I respected him. Then, in so many ways, I started to see him and do see him now in such a spiritual way.

This is a great man moving mountains with very little resources compared to his brother.

Joey Travolta has practically on his own brought so much awareness to Autism and is educating the world on this affliction that his nephew Jett had.

Can you imagine how hard it was on Joey when John refused his help regarding Jett, and was telling himself and the world his son had Kawasaki disease, all while his uncle Joey knew that he had Autism.

John outright refused to talk any further to Joey regarding Jett and they had a huge rift. With the love and understanding that Joey so desperately fought with his brother to give to his nephew, I believe Jett Travolta would be alive today.

You have to see what Joey Travolta's "Inline Productions" is doing with these kids with Autism. With Kelly and John's fame, they could have shared the truth about their son's condition with the world and embraced the gift God gave them to share about Jett.

But instead they stood by their religion's teachings, that Autism is unacceptable, so unacceptable their poor son was in their eyes, when a parent Photoshops pictures of their child to hide or mask their affliction, it can only be because of shame, I mean, can you imagine Photoshopping him into the child they wanted him to look like to the world?

I say, "Don't you just feel the love?"

The fight between the brothers idea of how to care for Jett's Autism was ultimately won by John, and unfortunately we all know how that ended up for poor little Jett.

Joey took his love for his neglected, improperly treated nephew and went out into the world and started to help all the other children out there with Autism who had parents that were completely different about their children's condition than John and Kelly....

They were not ashamed or in denial, they were simply looking for some hope for their Autistic child. No matter what Joey said to John it was always: 'no! I know what's best for Jett!'.

Joey had a run at acting and made his stamp in Hollywood as an actor in front of the camera, it is his life behind the camera and with the kids with Autism that is so beautiful. I have watched these kids completely come to life and be reinforced with these positive affirmations and actions with Joey as their hero and mentor.

Is it any wonder why I say he is the true star of that family. Jett Travolta could have blossomed through his uncle's love and been given a wonderful chance at a normal life, but John and Kelly said no.

In all families, there are sibling rivalries, but when it comes to the health and welfare of a child, I don't understand why they said no… Jett could be alive today if he had been allowed to be with his loving uncle. Only under oath did John Travolta finally admit that Jett suffered from Autism.

If that had all played out like it did with any other kid besides the Travoltas, they would have been charged with child neglect and endangerment.

Once again, Travolta was able to luckily escape the wrath of the media… which, by the way, was going in a very negative way for John and Kelly, but as usual they escaped.

If they had both taken the chance they were given with their child and shared his condition with the world, the world would have loved and rallied behind them.

I have found that on so many occasions when Travolta could have risen to the occasion of something positive besides his dick, he never did!

These truth are written in history already and the Internet has always been on top of what John and Kelly put their innocent boy through, all in the name of that ridiculous church that crazy nut L. Ron Hubbard started decades ago for out of luck and out of hope actors.

Joey Travolta is a man living his life to help others for the right reasons, he is a man to be honored and looked up too, if we could all take on something with such love and determination for change, it would be incredible.

The award for the brother who has lived his life for others and in honesty with no blatant lies about his life, is Joey Travolta, "The True Star Of The Travolta Family".

Joey's inclusion films, school and contact information can be reached in the following way:

Address: 146 Cypress Ave, Burbank, CA 91502

818-848-3708

JETT TRAVOLTA FOUNDATION

The Jett Travolta Foundation was set up by the deceased child's parents, in a pathetic attempt to turn all the attention away from the despicable inhumane way they treated their son Jett. People were outraged when they heard John and Kelly referring to their son's disease as "Kawasaki syndrome"...

They really must have thought that like all the things they have rewritten in their life, that they could now tell the world this wad of bullshit about Jett's condition, and we would believe it!!

How far can two people have their head up their ass? Would it be the correct question to how they handled the death of their son?

The media was not buying it and neither were their fans, the Internet was abuzz with everybody talking about what horrible parents they were for the way they treated Jett, and to deny him proper medication that would have stopped any seizures from killing him was absolute NEGLECT on both their parts. And then, to donate ten percent of the Jett Travolta Foundation to Scientology, the very church that had beliefs that killed him? It is so sad that Kelly and John did that to their child, only while on the witness stand in the Bahamas did John Travolta finally admit his son had Autism. Well, if that doesn't speak volumes on the kind of father Travolta was to his boy, I don't know what does!

For me to have witnessed Travolta in all the lewd acts I wrote about in "*You'll Never Spa In This Town Again*", the acts of homosexuality the very thing Scientology has no tolerance for, showed me up close and personal that he is a hypocrite all the way and a sexual predator.

As of the foundation's 2010-2011 tax returns, there had been not one dollar given to anybody or anything regarding Autism.

I used to cringe when I would hear Travolta describe how his son Jett got sick through all the carpet cleaning he did during those years, because he was such a clean freak (so he said). He was not such a clean freak while I witnessed him down on his knees in a dirty fungus-infested steam room sucking on a big fat black cock!

According to the website www.showbiz411.com, the foundation has given out $57,000.00 since conception?

WTF is what I say.

A father's love for his son sure shines through in black and white... Really, 57K when you have so many millions? Seems to me he should have established Jett's Foundation with a minimum of one million dollars. But as I have already stated this foundation was Travolta's answer to a PR crisis, not a beloved son's death! And the proof is in public domain.

To have actually witnessed **firsthand** Travolta's mistreatment of his son was utterly disturbing, to say the least. I knew then when John was inside the spa masturbating with this guy and getting their germ-infested sauna love on, that he was an unfit father and if the authorities had witnessed his behavior that day, Travolta would have made world news with a sex arrest with his son with him...

He really lucked out again that day.... Can you imagine when George Michael was arrested in Beverly Hills that infamous day, if he had had a 16 year old relative with him, on the day of sexual bathroom cruising? Or if Pee Wee Herman's infamous sex arrest for playing with himself in public at that movie theater---can you imagine if he had had a 16 year old relative along with him?

Well that is exactly what daddy John Travolta did! When I witnessed his parenting skills on January 11 2007, he was hooking up in a public spa while his son was with him…

That was a very sad day, to witness that little lost boy looking for his missing father, who was busy in the spa…sad.

It would be great to see in time the Jett Travolta Foundation really stand for something good and true, but that day will never really come… this smoke screen they established after Jett's death will fade into the dark, like their poor child did while left alone for so many hours in that bathroom on that fatal night.

Just as these years now since Jett's death have proven, very little interest or love coming out of this foundation. The truth we saw was the immediate alleged pregnancy of Kelly Preston. I do believe they had a baby, but I know that she did not deliver or carry that baby herself.

Anyway, to replace a child just like that shows you how this couple thinks. I can only hope by the time baby Benjamin is Jett's age that his Father will have stopped his sexual addiction that made him make so many wrong choices with Jett.

JAMES GANDOLFINI…..

I awoke the other day to GMA and Travolta was on it, he had to be there he was doing required press for his upcoming movie with Robert DeNiro…*A Killing Season..*

They brought up Gandolfini's passing and John jumped right in with how it was so sad and that he was Galdofini's inspiration to become an actor. Travolta went on to say his father had sold tires to Gandolfini's father and they basically grew up near each other.

Travolta then went on to tell the most touching story about Gandolfini, and how he had shown up at Travolta's home in Florida unannounced to stay with John and Kelly for five days and nights right after their son Jett had passed away days earlier…

I was so touched to hear that Gandolfini was so loving and caring and that he took it upon himself to show up to help the Travolta's during their worst of days… the days following Jett's death. Travolta then went on to boast how he would be there for the boy Gandolfini's son…

"I will personally be there for the boy and make sure he is taken care of."

He didn't even know or remember Gandolfini's son's name! (So Travolta)

He only cares when the camera is rolling.

All the hosts---Robin Givens, George Stephanopoulos, etc., were listening to Travolta go on and on about how he will personally make this better.

Travolta couldn't tell the sweet story first about Gandolfini coming out to stay first when he was talking. No, he had to jump right in with "I was his inspiration to become an actor" again!

"So Travolta" and so self consumed...

I would hope after all these decades of people fondling Travolta's ego, he would finally be somewhat full! But no... He is so empty as a newborn for milk....

Helen Travolta, John's mother, would truly be ashamed of her son if she saw all the things I have seen her son do in public.

I watched the funeral on TV and as I expected, NO JOHN TRAVOLA in attendance... Prior obligations!! As always!

I would have thought that not only would Travolta attend the funeral, (especially since he cashed in on it on all the shows) during his film's PR obligations...

For sure, even if you have an ironclad reason why you couldn't be there, why wouldn't you send your wife Kelly and daughter Ella in your place to represent the Travolta family's support, especially since Travolta was announcing to the world that HE personally was going to look after this family... This is the true Travolta!

Wednesday, June 26, 2013 was Gandolfini's wake and viewing for those close to him, again no Travolta, but Travolta did spend that day with his son riding a train and having fun.

Thursday June 27, 2013 was the funeral and I'm sure you know by now Travolta was not there in any way or form, instead he was at the Breittani watch opening... and cutting the ribbon of the store. After what Gandolfini did for both John and Kelly, this is how they express their final gratitude for the man.

There is only one thing Travolta has on his mind and it is not paying respect for anyone or anything. If I were wrong you would have seen Travolta and Wife at the services, but you didn't, the good thing is you gotta know they were not missed.

We all know that Travolta has several planes and can and has flown across the world on a whim... and yet he couldn't make it to James Gandolfini's final day? "I mean after all, John inspired him to become an actor!"

Just like Liberace lied to the world all his life, so has Travolta, and like Liberace, it all comes out one way or another in the end.

I never saw one episode of the Sopranos, I did know of Gandolfini from his Sopranos fame, but I had never seen him act, then one night I saw him with Robert Redford in "White Castles", I was spellbound from the moment Gandolfini came on screen, and I couldn't take my eyes off of his performance.

The next day, I told a lot of my friends about this amazing actor I had never seen before who blew me away with his performance. I watched the film many times after that, and every time with Gandolfini, it felt like the first time I was seeing it.

He was an amazing actor and John Travolta should have lived up to what he was telling the world about being there for the Gandolfini family, instead, the Travoltas were a no-show.

QUEEN LATIFAH TV SHOW DEBUT SEPTEMBER 16, 2013...

I have always liked Queen Latifah, and I used to think that she was the kind of women that would stand for truth and honesty.

Many of us in the LGBT community have known for years that she is gay, because we have seen her doing her thing at Gay Pride with her girlfriend being gay...

I wonder why it is so hard for her to say it? I mean she partakes in "Our", meaning LGBT, events and openly enjoys being gay out and about, yet she won't say it... hum...

As I said I used to like her! To me she's in the same category as Travolta, it was so fitting that he would be her first guest... The closeted homosexual and the closeted Lesbian talk show host.

Queen Latifah has been quoted as saying she does not discuss her personal life, it is hers and that is that! Bull shit!! She gave up her personal privacy a long time ago when she stepped into the spotlight.and renamed herself "Queen" How convenient for her that she can play straight and get cover girl deals and TV shows...

She is not the women I thought she was... She is certainly NO Ellen DeGeneres... Ellen is a woman that at the early height of her career she told the world that she was gay.

Can you imagine all the people on this earth that Ellen touched in ways known only to them and God?

Like Travolta, Queen Latifah is a hypocrite!

And no friend to the LGBT community.

Make no mistake, she will officially come out someday. But it will only be when she has lied to us all on a daily basis of "who" she truly is...

I mean if you're going to have a talk show, shouldn't it start with a host who is honest to us in all manners of her life... not like Latifah did today on her show, talking about guys and winking like she might like to hit it? How stupid does she think we are...

I predict that her show will be dropped soon enough for many reasons, but the number one reason is you can tell when you look at her that she is not an open, honest women... she is covered, and protected?

When people are like that, it is because they have a reason or something to hide. She might have had a better chance of making it, had she opened her first show with the announcement that we all know she is long overdue for...

My guess is she might try and do it later to save the show when it starts to go away, but it will be too late...The concept of her show is fake, she is a fake, and her first guest is the world's number one homosexual fake, her producers must think were back in the days of "The Donna Reed Show".

She had the platform to change the world, and yet she only focused on changing her bank account... I say goodbye!!

The world will eventually tune out to this phoney baloney woman and her show.

Until then, keep in mind, everyday she lives her life as she does (In The Closet), she is selling out the LGBT community.

Her latest ad for her show reads. "Queen Latifah up close and personal"... She's a hypocrite, just like her first guest, Travolta!

"A Society that tolerates Homosexuality and all its attendant perversions does not deserve to exist."

L. Ron Hubbard, 1950

Hubbard said it and published it, making it
UNALTERABLE DOCTRINE

This is exactly how Adolf Hitler felt about
Our community

"Scientology is not Homophobic
in any way,
in fact, it's one of the more tolerant
faiths."

John Travolta   2007

Top
Member of Scientology
For
39…YEARS!

COMING SOON

"HITLERS SECRET LGBT HOLOCAUST"

I know the secret!

DO YOU
?

If you're "LGBT," you should!

TRAVOLTA ENCOUNTER….DECEMBER, 2001

THE MAIN REASON I DECIDED TO NEVER TOUCH TRAVOLTA.

I received so many emails from people who had read my book and many of them were not buying the fact that I would go through so much mental and physical transformation to meet Travolta and then not have sex with him? Well, I knew when I was writing it, people would think I was crazy for not going through with full on sex…

After all, as one person wrote, "You spent so many years transforming yourself to be John Travolta's boyfriend, and then you just glide over the whole issue in your book? I, for one, think something has been left out."

Well, she was right, I did leave something out, something "Huge" that made me close the door on hooking up with the man of my desires, the great and powerful Travolta. It was something pretty simple, but it hit me like a ton of bricks.

About six months earlier, I had come across a vendor at a flea market who had a collection of "LGBT Holocaust Armbands" that he was selling and within a few months I had purchased all the artifacts that represent the lives lost in the Holocaust, this was big for the LGBT community, I knew that right away…

I felt compelled to share these artifacts with the world, so on December 16, 2000, I rented a retail shop at 616 N Doheny Drive in West Hollywood, to do a window for the holidays, with my message that the true first hate crime against LGBTs was in Hitler's Holocaust.

It was going to be like the holiday windows they do in New York during the holidays. My window of compassion for the LGBT community, spreading awareness of LGBTs in the Holocaust.

I put the artifacts in the window along with a poem and images of the lives lost in the Holocaust. It really took off and before I knew it, the media was covering it and people were flocking to it in groves.

I really felt I had done something right to spread awareness in the LGBT community about our past. I always say, "You can't know where you're going… If you don't know where you've been," and the fact that LGBTs had suffered so horribly in the Holocaust was news to me.

Just months before my historic purchase, I really had no clue that LGBTs were in the Holocaust and that they were treated the absolute worst.

My holiday window had taken off and people were talking and I was doing everything I could to keep it going---this is where Travolta comes in.

Everybody at City Spa caught wind of my window for the Holocaust armbands and they were going to see the window and pay their respects for the dead victims, and when the Los Angeles Times did their story, things got really busy at the store front.

I saw Travolta at the spa one afternoon during this time and I asked him if he would go to the window with Kelly and the kids and let me take a photograph to show that the Travoltas had stopped by to look at the artifacts and pay their respects this holiday season, but that is not what happened.

When I saw Travolta, I mustered up my courage to ask him if he would do this not for me but for humanity, he replied back to me, "I'm not going anywhere near that LGBT display of yours in West Hollywood, I don't owe the LGBTs anything and I sure as hell am not going to be photographed at some gay spot."

I was I shock with those harsh words of his about the LGBT community, after all, he is gay!

He knows, I know he is and for him to say those words to me made no sense, so I asked him, "What do you call yourself when you are hooking up with all these men for sex, aren't you gay as well?" And he replied "I'll never admit it."

WHAT A HYPOCRITE, I thought.

Here he is at these spas, having sex with all these men out in the open and he denies that he is gay and he feels he doesn't owe anything to the LGBT community.

For him to belong to Scientology and be its number one advocate besides Tom Cruise, when they believe 100 percent that Homosexuality is not accepted and then for him to parade around like a male whore at these spas and then try to pass himself off as straight was beyond weird, but that is what it was.

He, of course, never came to the window to try and help the cause in any way, shape or form.

He will partake in the benefits of being a homosexual, but he will go to every length to deny it in every way to pull the wool over the world's eyes.

He looked at me, and said, "Fuck the faggots and the Holocaust!"

From that moment on, I could not stand to be near the man and in fact, over the next several years that I have chronicled in my last book, "YNSITTA". I went out of my way to avoid the man, but you know with people who have diseases, they can't help their behavior??? Yeah, right!

It was very clear to me that the LGBT community was OK for us to be his loyal movie paying fans, and he liked that, but he thought all LGBTs as less than him, even though he, too, is gay, it must be because of his Scientology teachings? Yeah, right!

The message I was spreading that holiday season did just fine without the help of the hypocrite Travolta. I would never look at him the same again, although to be quite honest with you, by this time I already knew I would never let him put his lips on my dick, I had seen him have so much unprotected sex that it made me fear for my clean HIV status, so I had already made up my mind that this guy was not for me, but his hatred for the LGBT community just sealed the deal for me.

Travolta could have been an inspiration to young LGBTs all around the world, but he missed that chance, just like he missed the chance to spread awareness about Autism with his son Jett, instead he and Kelly lied to the world for years saying Jett had "Kawasaki disease" and kept him either hidden or Photoshopped when out, and as you can see, the world is learning more every day about Autism and we are doing just fine again without the Travoltas…

Subject: John Travolta
From: XXXXXXXXX
Date: June 23, 2013
To: info@youllneverspainthistownagain.com

Hello Randolph,

I have plenty to share regarding Travolta and his latest boyfriend.

Do you pay for the stories you write about or are there by donation?

I would like to be paid for my story. I can prove the truth of it for you and show you some pictures that will clear up any doubt you may ponder.

I have contacted the National Enquirer, but they are giving me the run around regarding payment. If you would like to take advantage of this opportunity, contact me soon.

I have a very interesting sex story to share with you for the right price to me. I have photographic proof to show you I am for real. Not interested in wasting your time or mine.

April 3, 2013, is a day that Travolta was in town while his wife shot parts of her TV pilot. On this particular day, I had a chance meeting with him.

What happened that day is worth the money to hear... trust me!

I am interested in being paid, but do not want to put my name to the story. As you can imagine, it would be the end of my career. I work in the business as well.

I have a few other celebrity stories I can share with you as well, but I really think you will be excited to get a hold of these Travolta details for your book.

Please let me know ASAP.

Subject: Travolta
From: XXXXXXXXXXX
Date: July 10, 2013
To: info@youllneverspainthistownagain.com

Hiya. I came across your web site and your information about John Travolta. I found it interesting and truthful. I say truthful, because I've had a couple of hookups with the actor myself. I live in Santa Monica, CA. I really don't get what the deal is with him anyway?

I first met Mr. Travolta a few years ago when I was an extra on a film. He was working on a movie called Savages. He was a lot of fun to hang out with and make out with, too. Believe you me.

I met him the first day of shooting and, after a few days of flirting back and forth, we eventually hooked up. I'm not writing you to share a bunch of dirty details about a nasty fuck fest although that's EXACTLY what we had, LOL, instead I'm writing to say I think it's a sad situation the actor is in. Sad because, obviously, he is not a happy man.

I ran into John at Century Spa this year on July 29, 2013. He was in the sauna having a steam, when I walked in and recognized him. He noticed me immediately as well.

We spoke about Savages and what we both thought about the final cut. He said he wasn't happy about the ending. He also stated that Oliver Stone was an ass to him most of the time. Seemed to me, Travolta was in a sad place with his life.

I was really hoping to have another round with him in the bedroom, but that was not to be. We had a very quick meet and greet on our knees and then he said he had to take off. We both showered and kept talking as we headed to the lockers to get dressed.

When we got outside to the parking lot, we were parked practically next to each other. He was driving an old blue Mercedes Benz. He gave me a nod… and drove off.

I think he is a very unhappy man and it's just so sad to see him like that.

I appreciate your time,

Sincerely,

XXXXXXXX

From: francine S xxxxxxxxxxxxxxxx
To: robbyrandolph <robbyrandolph@aol.com> .
Subject: do you know about this? how is the book coming?
XOXOXOXOXOXOXOXO!!!!!!!!!
Date: Fri, Feb 28, 2014 12:49 am

318. BLIND GOSSIP 02/27 **#1 **

Warning: The following blind item is definitely NSFW (Not Safe For Work)! There have been lots of stories in the past about this superstar actor's chronic misbehavior with massage therapists and the legal cases that have been quietly settled following those encounters. Well, we have another one for you... and this one is the most shocking yet!

This case has not yet been resolved, but there are a few interesting (and quite gross) details about it that make it different from the other cases we have heard about. This massage therapist was called to a hotel room to give a massage to an unidentified guest.

When he arrived, he was surprised to discover that the guest was a world-famous actor. The massage therapist set up a table and the actor got on the table and lay on his stomach. Then it got... weird.

The actor began moaning and humping the table after a few minutes. When he turned over, he had a huge erection and began masturbating in front of the massage therapist. He grabbed the massage therapist's package... and then ejaculated all over the jeans that the massage therapist was wearing!

Now here are the three twists: One: The massage therapist's jeans got the Monica Lewinsky treatment!

The shocked massage therapist saved the pants --- which had been sprayed with the actor's semen --- and sent them to a laboratory to prove that it was the actor's DNA.

Two: There was a third person in the room during this entire encounter! The actor actually brought along someone to film the action! Apparently, the actor has an entire collection of videos of himself jerking off.

Three: The person who was filming the action? The actor's family nanny! Yes, when not busy caring for the actor's children, the actor has the Nanny serve as an amateur porn videographer. Nice parenting there.

Needless to say, the massage therapist was wigging out during this entire encounter. While he actually wants the case to go to trial, it will likely get settled quietly, with the details of the actor's depravity once again swept under the rug. *John Travolta*

From: robbyrandolph <robbyrandolph@aol.com>
To: Francine S xxxxxxxxxxxxx
Subject: Re: do you know about this? how is the book coming? XOXOXOXOXOXOXOXO!!!!!!!!
Date: Sun, Mar 2,2014 1:34 PM

No! I had not seen this.

I appreciate you forwarding it to me, seems like old times ... LOL.

I've heard a lot of CRAZY things about him but this is really weird...

Whatever it is true or false, it keeps the thought of his actions out there... He reallly is a horrible guy with all he has done to sooooo many men...

Are you watching the Academy awards?? We are...

Glad to hear from you... Anything you might see on him, please send to me ... 1 think it is gonna be quiet for a minute...

I'm almost there with the book.... Thanks for asking... I am not going to give up...

Your xxxxx

"The contention that my client would engage in adultery in a spa where he could be witnessed by a third party even once, would be dubious at best."

Marty Singer,
John Travolta's Attorney

THE

END

For now!

ACKNOWLEDGEMENTS

I want to thank all the people who took the time out of their busy day to reach out to me and encourage me to continue with my story! It was very touching to hear from so many beautiful souls.

I want to thank all the men that reached out to me for help regarding Travolta. I hope in some way my speaking up for you and telling your stories you feel a little closure and can look to a brighter day. By telling me your stories and allowing me the privilege to include them in this book, you are my heroes.

To Ocy Hinkle, without your constant support and availability to listen and help guide me… I really think there would be no "Tracking Travolta". You knew this was a burning desire of mine to help these men and because of you, I was able too. I remain in constant awe of your abilities to turn my ideas into realities.

Charles Karpinski, my personal angel from God. I will never know what I did so right to have earned a lifetime of your love and friendship, but I do know this…I love you forever! "Our" time we spent together as partners was certainly eighteen amazing years of joy and happiness. That is always in my heart. I Thank God for you, Chuck!!

To my friend Terry Lane, I was blessed the day I met you so many moons ago, what fun two friends had without a care in the world back then. You have always been the grown up! I have always looked up to you, and to have witnessed firsthand the love you have for everyone around you is amazing. You continue to inspire me with your strength and courage and friendship!

To G. Scott Sobel, Esq. Your counsel and friendship is priceless to me! Through you, I witness a man living his life with integrity and compassion for others. After spending years in the real estate business, I had lost all faith in "Business Men". Nobody even remembered what a thing like ethics was… Then I met you! What a breath of fresh air you are. I look up to you my friend and aspire to be at a level "closer" to yours someday.

To Sarah Golden, Esq. You told me so many lies at our final "Travolta" meeting you should be ashamed of yourself. You sold Fabian out! The truth will shine through on your actions.

To Fabian Zanzi, "Surprise!". I hope I made you happy with bringing your story to the world "Again." I hope you have a wonderful life and in time, the name John Travolta will be nothing but an old memory…You were always so much more than what he did to you….Have a beautiful life, my friend!. The rest of your story is coming soon.

To Chris Williams, I hope you always remember you are a great guy full of love and humor. I tried my best to tell your story and let the world know what Travolta did to you.

To Francine Smiderly, I have been blessed with your friendship and undying loyalty to me. Your tireless efforts and research are appreciated more than you know!

To Lorrie V. Llamas

I saved the best for last! To the dearest friend I was blessed to live with for five glorious, peaceful, beyond happy years.

If it had not been for your love, I would not be here today, Lorrie. God knew what he was doing when he brought your love to me.

"You rescued me" and though you're not here in the physical form, you continue to guide me with your beautiful whispers of love you speak to me. This book would not exist if you had not urged me to start writing the first one "YNSITTA".

You brought me back to life and I love you for it. I hope you're happy with the way I'm "Holding Down The Fort." Thank you for leaving me with a reason to get up every day and face a new day…

Dali n Dazi…'n the birds too!

The two dogs I bought for you have become my life, and they continue to be a living breathing direct link to the greatest friend a person could ever possibly have…"YOU!"

I love you Lorrie, and miss you with each day! …Until we're "All" together again, please know Dali 'n Dazi 'n Dadi are loving you… Your family lives on!

www.ingramcontent.com/pod-product-compliance
Lightning Source LLC
Chambersburg PA
CBHW061632040426
42446CB00010B/1381